Industrial Britain

The Workshop of the World

Christine Counsell
Director of Social Studies
John Cabot CTC Bristol

and

Chris Steer
Deputy Headteacher
Rednock School

CAMBRIDGE
UNIVERSITY PRESS

Published by the Press Syndicate of the University of Cambridge
The Pitt Building, Trumpington Street, Cambridge CB2 1RP
40 West 20th Street, New York, NY 10011–4211, USA
10 Stamford Street, Oakleigh, Melbourne 3166, Australia

First published 1993

Printed in Great Britain at the University Press, Cambridge

A catalogue record for this book is available from the British Library

ISBN 0 521 42494 1 paperback

Designed and produced by Gecko Limited, Bicester, Oxon
Picture research by Linda Proud
Illustrations by Jon Blake, John Plumb, Chris Rothero,
William Rowsell, Martin Sanders and Sue Shields

Notice to teachers
Many of the sources used in this textbook have been adapted or abridged from
the original.

Cover illustration: *'The Dinner Hour, Wigan'*, 1874 by Eyre Crowe, Manchester City Art
Galleries

Acknowledgements
The author and publisher would like to thank the following for permission to reproduce
the illustrations on the following pages:

Bridgeman Art Library, London 4–5, 8, 17, 22–23 (bottom), 24, 27, 31, 35, 49, 54, 57, 60,
64–65, 66, 70, 72–73 (bottom), 75, 76, 82; Collections, London 92; ET Archive, London 13,
59, 71 (top); Mary Evans Picture Library, London 6–7, 20, 22 (top), 23 (top), 25, 26, 28, 29,
30, 33 (top left), 34 (top right), 43, 62, 63, 72–73 (top), 77, 83; Ferens Art Gallery, Kingston-
upon-Hull 38; Fine Art Photographic Library, London 68, 74 (top); Fotomas, Beckingham,
Kent 90–91; John Gorman, Waltham Abbey 51; Sally and Richard Greenhill, London 93;
Harris Art Gallery, Preston 67; Hulton-Deutsch Picture Company, London 52, 71 (bottom), 87;
Institute of Agricultural History, University of Reading 14 (bottom), 15 (top); Mansell
Collection, London 42, 44, 53, 62–63 (top); Peter Hollings, Halifax 55; National Portrait
Gallery, London 33 (top right), 33 (bottom right), 34 (centre), 88; Oxford Central Library
Photographic Archive 74 (bottom); The Punch Library 54 (top); Royal Borough of Kensington
and Chelsea, Leighton House Museum 69; The Royal Collection, by courtesy of HM the
Queen 16; Skyscan, Glos. 12–13; Sir John Soanes Museum, London 81; Tate Gallery, London
14 (top).

Contents

Introduction: The Great Exhibition

Britain went through enormous changes between 1750 and 1900 and became the world's first industrial nation. In the summer of 1851 an enormous display of industrial goods was held in London. This Great Exhibition was a celebration of the new factories that had been built and the industrial changes that had taken place in the past century.

What can we learn from the Great Exhibition about Britain at the time?

Britain exhibits her greatness

The Great Exhibition of 1851 was the idea of Queen Victoria's husband, Prince Albert. It became an opportunity for British manufacturers to show off their goods and the quality of their craftsmanship. The exhibition displayed over 100,000 items and these showed how Britain clearly led the world in technology and engineering. The exhibition was held in a magnificent building called the Crystal Palace (Source A). During the six months that it was open, over 6 million people visited the Great Exhibition to marvel at the progress that had been made since the eighteenth century. It was not only the rich who visited; some factory owners even gave their workers a day off and paid for both the trip and the admission. Ordinary people were able to get to London from all over the country using the newly-opened railways.

A vision of progress

The Great Exhibition naturally led many people to admire the enormous achievements of British industry. It encouraged people to be proud of the rapid progress that had been made. We can find many examples of talk and comment about such improvement and progress.

Source A

The Crystal Palace in Hyde Park. It was made entirely of glass and iron. The exhibits ranged from industrial machinery to household goods.

- *What does this building suggest about the importance that was attached to the Great Exhibition?*

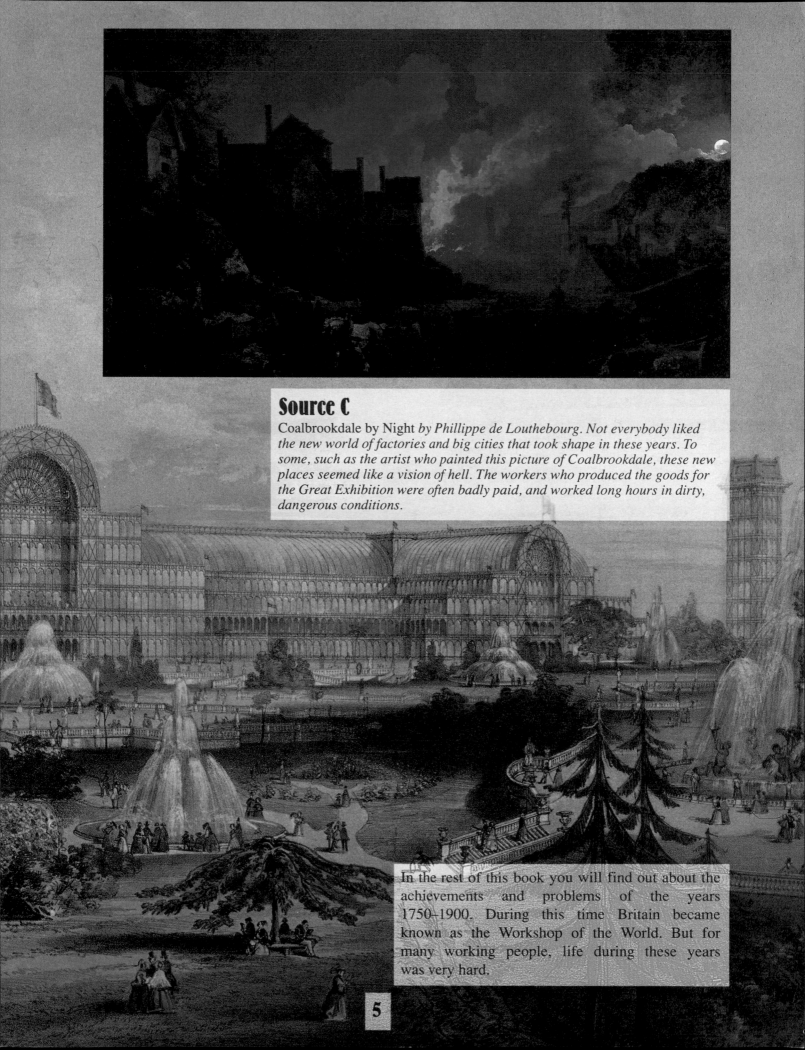

Source C

Coalbrookdale by Night *by Phillippe de Louthebourg. Not everybody liked the new world of factories and big cities that took shape in these years. To some, such as the artist who painted this picture of Coalbrookdale, these new places seemed like a vision of hell. The workers who produced the goods for the Great Exhibition were often badly paid, and worked long hours in dirty, dangerous conditions.*

In the rest of this book you will find out about the achievements and problems of the years 1750–1900. During this time Britain became known as the Workshop of the World. But for many working people, life during these years was very hard.

THE Workshop

The population grew quickly

Between 1750 and 1900 the number of people living in the British Isles increased more rapidly than ever before. In 1750 there were about 10 million people; in 1900 there were 40 million people. This created a huge demand for food, clothing and houses. Many businessmen and farmers became rich by providing for this growing population.

Farming is improved

Farmers became more efficient. They were able to make bigger profits by providing food for the growing population. However, although farmers grew rich, farm workers were very badly paid.

Industry

After 1750 British industry grew rapidly. It was particularly successful in making cotton goods, in making iron and steel and in mining coal. Britain's engineering also led the world for most of the nineteenth century. By 1851 Britain could truly be called the 'workshop of the world'.

Power

In 1750 Britain's energy needs were provided for by the use of wind, wood, water and animals. By 1900 most power depended on the use of coal: four tonnes of coal were used in each year for every man, woman and child. The development of steam power had transformed transport and industry.

Factory system

In 1750 most people in manufacturing worked in their own homes or in small workshops. Very little large machinery was used. The growing use of water and then steam power meant that large numbers of workers could be employed in one place. In the nineteenth century large factories became more common.

The world's merchant

Britain was an important trading country before 1750. Its goods were sold to Europe, America, Africa and Asia. After 1750 the value of Britain's trade grew rapidly: between 1750 and 1900 the value of Britain's exports grew 15 times. Ports such as Bristol, Liverpool and Glasgow grew in size and wealth.

Britain's Empire

In 1750 Britain already possessed colonies. The most important of these were in North America and the West Indies. After a war with France, Britain won control of India. Although the USA won its independence in 1783, the Empire continued to grow. By 1900 nearly 400 million people and one-fifth of the world's land were ruled by Britain.

Transport

The speed of travel changed dramatically after 1750, when the average speed on a long journey had been only four miles per hour. Better roads, new canals and, above all, the railways meant that people and goods could move much more quickly. The journey from Edinburgh to London had once taken seven days or more. In 1900 the same journey took ten hours.

1 Population growth and urbanisation

Many of the changes in Britain between 1750 and 1900 were linked to a great increase in population. The sources in this unit show you when, where and by how much the population grew.

What happened to Britain's population between 1750 and 1900?

Population

One of the most basic changes that took place in Britain between 1750 and 1900 was a huge increase in population. There were nearly five times as many people at the end of the period than at the beginning. At the same time there was a move from the country-side to the towns. Between 1750 and 1800 the population of Manchester increased from 18,000 to 90,000 people.

No one is quite sure why the British population started to increase dramatically after 1750. It used to be thought that improved medicine reduced the death rate. Recently historians have decided that there is little evidence to support this. Instead they think that there was a rise in the number of babies being born.

During the eighteenth century the proportion of the population who were unmarried fell and women got married slightly earlier. These changes in marriage led to a rise in the birth rate.

The rise in population and the move to the cities played a part in the other changes of this period. More babies eventually meant more workers for the new industries that developed after 1750. A larger population also led to a rise in the demand for food and factory goods. People in towns and cities did not make their own food and clothes in the way that many country people did, so the move to the cities encouraged people to spend more money in the shops.

The Family of Alfrederick Smith Hatch, 1871 *by J. Eastman Johnson.*

Source A

These figures show how and when the population of the British Isles grew:

Year	England	Wales	Scotland	Ireland	Totals
1701	5,100,000	450,000	1,000,000	2,700,000	9,250,000
1751	5,800,000	500,000	1,200,000	3,200,000	10,700,000
1801	8,700,000	600,000	1,600,000	5,000,000	15,900,000
1851	16,800,000	1,200,000	2,900,000	6,500,000	27,400,000
1871	21,300,000	1,400,000	3,400,000	5,400,000	31,500,000
1901	30,500,000	2,000,000	4,500,000	4,500,000	41,500,000

John Wilkes, *United Kingdom: A Social and Economic History of Modern Britain*, 1984

Source B

Pie charts showing changes in the balance of population between towns and country-side in Great Britain:

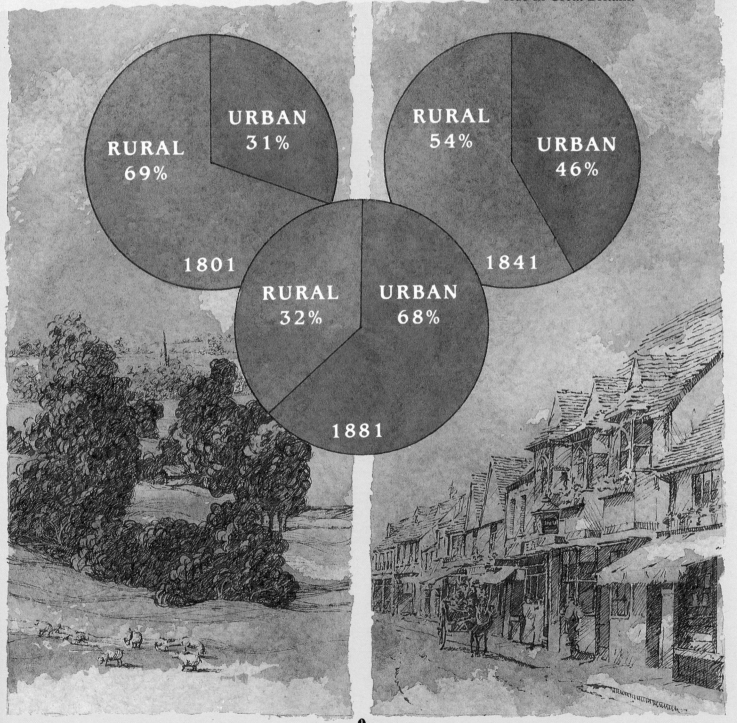

RURAL 69% URBAN 31% 1801

RURAL 54% URBAN 46% 1841

RURAL 32% URBAN 68% 1881

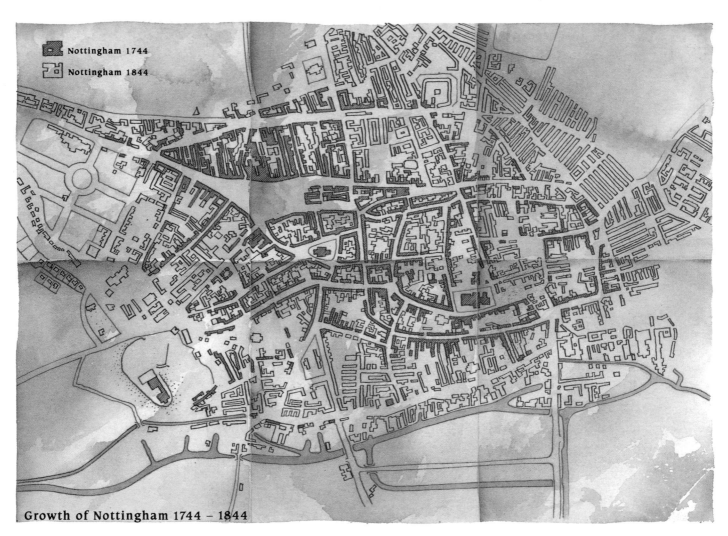

Growth of Nottingham 1744 – 1844

Nottingham 1744
Nottingham 1844

Source C

This map based on original maps produced in 1744 and 1844 shows the changes which occurred in the city of Nottingham, over a period of 100 years.

Source D

Population and living space in Nottingham, 1779–1851.

60
55
50 — Population in thousands
45
40
35
30
25
20
15
10
5

2000
1800
1600
1400
1200
1000
800
600
400
200

Acres

1739   1793   1811   1831   1851

---

1 Look carefully at the plan of Nottingham.
a What are the main differences between the Nottingham of 1744 and Nottingham in 1844?
b What suggestions can you make about how the lives of the people of Nottingham might have changed as a result of these differences?

2 What happened to the population of Britain between 1750 and 1900? Use information from the sources to support the points that you make.

2 Changes in farming

Throughout this period more people were employed on farms and in jobs based on farming, such as milling or brewing, than in any other single type of job. Farming became much more efficient during these years but historians disagree about how this happened.

Why did the output of farms rise?

An increase in output

British farming slowly became more and more efficient between 1650 and 1850. This meant that, although the total amount of land was largely fixed, farmers were able to produce more and more food from this land area.

Source A

A modern British historian considers how farming changed:

'Total corn output rose from about 13 million quarters (a quarter is 28 lb) in 1700 to nearly 15 million in 1750, to 19 million in 1800, and 25 million in 1820. The numbers of sheep increased from 11 million in 1688 to 26 million by 1820. The weight of individual cattle rose by about one quarter between 1700 and 1820.'

P. Mathias, *The First Industrial Nation*, 1983 edition

Improved efficiency

These agricultural improvements were very important. They meant that more food would be available as more and more people moved to towns and started to work in factories. How did the farmers improve their efficiency? Over the years people have come up with a number of explanations for this change. These explanations include:

the impact of enclosure
new approaches to arable farming
new ways of breeding animals
new machines

- Using information from this unit, work out whether you think these factors were important.

11

This aerial photograph shows the effects of enclosure on the traditional strip-farming method of agriculture.

Enclosure

In the Middle Ages many villages had their land divided into two or three enormous fields. Each field was sub-divided into a great number of tiny strips. Each farmer would have strips scattered across the fields. In the period 1500–1750 many of these open fields were enclosed – reorganised into more compact, hedged fields. There was a further increase in enclosure from 1750 onwards.

A government report in 1794 revealed many of the problems associated with traditional methods of farming:

- Progressive farmers had little chance to try new methods because, since *all* the farmers had to agree to any changes, an obstinate tenant had the power to stop any improvements.

- A farmer's land could be scattered over a large common field which meant that he had to travel two or three miles to visit it all.

- It was impossible for farmers to try to improve their animal breeds when the animals were mixed in with those of their neighbours.

After enclosure many rough grazing areas were ploughed up and on enclosed land the amount of grain produced from a field often increased. Both these factors led to more food being produced. However, the scale of enclosure was limited. Only in the English Midlands was there a very intensive move to enclosure in the years after 1750. In Ireland, Scotland and Wales most farms had always been enclosed and even in England only about a quarter of the land was actually enclosed between 1750 and 1900 – the rest had been enclosed earlier.

Changes in arable farming

In the Middle Ages farmers regularly left fields without planted crops once every three or four years. This was called leaving fields fallow. In the eighteenth century many farmers abandoned this approach and, instead, used a rotation of different crops each year. In this way more land was kept in use and extra feed was grown for animals.

Source C

The most famous crop rotation of the years 1750–1900 was the Norfolk rotation made popular by the writer Arthur Young:

> 'No fortune will be made by farming unless a sound rotation of crops is used. That which has been chiefly adopted by the Norfolk farmers is:
> 1 turnips 3 clover
> 2 barley 4 wheat'

Arthur Young, 1771

To enrich the soil and grow more crops farmers made more use of a method called marling. This involved mixing in clay on light sandy soils. On heavy clay soils farmers got a similar effect by adding chalk or lime.

Selective breeding

Influenced by the growing interest in pedigree horses and dogs, many farmers also took an interest in the selective breeding of farm animals. One of the most famous of these new breeders was Robert Bakewell. He managed to produce a new, larger sheep called the New Leicester. This sheep had a long fleece and produced a lot of mutton. Between 1700 and 1800 the weight of farm animals at Smithfield Market more than doubled.

Mr Healey's Sheep
by W. H. Davies.

Source D *Jethro Tull's seed drill.*

New machines

In the first half of the eighteenth century Jethro Tull invented a seed drill which sowed seeds in straight lines and covered them up in one operation. Previously seed had been sown broadcast which meant that it was simply thrown onto the surface of the earth by hand. What advantages would Tull's method have?

In the nineteenth century ploughs continued to be improved. Machines for threshing corn had begun to be developed in the 1790s. At first these were powered by hand or by horse. In the nineteenth century steam power was adapted to provide the power for much farm machinery, including ploughs and threshing machines.

How great were the changes in farming?

What can we learn from the following sources about the way farming changed between 1750 and 1900?

Source F
The Haymakers
*by George Stubbs,
1785.*

Source G
*Haymaking in the
Cotswolds in the
1880s.*

BARLEY ▸ TURNIPS
CLOVER ▸ WHEAT

Source H

An advertisement for farm machinery, 1897.

● *What different types of machine can you see? Why do you think that not all farmers used these machines?*

Source I

The writer of this source grew up in a village in north Oxfordshire. Here she describes the use of machines in the 1880s:

'Machinery was just coming into use on the land. Every autumn appeared a pair of large traction engines. Such machinery as the farmer owned was horse-drawn and was only in partial use. In some fields a horse-drawn drill would sow the seed in rows, in others a human sower would walk up and down with a basket and fling the seed with both hands broadcast. In harvest time, the mechanical reaper was a familiar sight, but it only did a small part of the work.'

Flora Thompson, *Lark Rise to Candleford*

1 Read Source A. What does it tell us about how farming changed between 1700 and 1820?

2 a Explain how each of these factors led to more food being produced:
enclosure   new ways of breeding animals
new machines   crop rotations
b Give each of these four factors a score out of 10 (ranging from 0 = not important to 10 = very important) to show how important you think it was. Explain your answer.

3 Look at Sources F, G and I, noting the date of each source. What do they tell us about change in the countryside in the nineteenth century?

3 The birth of the factory

A great change took place in the cotton industry in the last quarter of the eighteenth century. Instead of making cotton thread in people's houses, manufacturers set up new factories. This was the beginning of the factory age.

Why did the cotton industry start using factories?

The importance of cotton

Woollen cloth had been made in Britain for many centuries. This work was usually done in small workshops or in people's cottages. By the time Source A was painted, the large factories in which textiles were produced had changed the face of Britain and cotton had become much more important than wool. Exports of cotton goods were worth only £11,000 per year in the 1740s but this had risen to £17 million by 1820. By 1850 cotton goods were the leading British export.

Source A
A View of Manchester *by Wyld, 1851.*

Source B – Cottage industry
Cotton hand-spinning in Ireland in the eighteenth century. This is the downstairs room of the cottage. The spinning wheels would be pushed into a corner when the family wanted to eat.

Source C – A cut-away diagram of a cotton factory
Before the invention of steam power, factories and mills depended on fast-flowing rivers to turn water wheels which provided the power for all the machines. This drawing shows how the water wheel operated a series of pulleys, belts and overhead lines which were connected to individual machines.

Historians have often argued about why Britain was able to become the first industrial nation. Here are some possible reasons why the changes in the textile industry took place:

1 The population was increasing and therefore the demand for textiles was growing. The population of the British Isles went from nearly 10.7 million in 1750 to over 27.4 million in 1850. Producers of textiles knew they could get rich by producing more goods. Do you think that Britain's population increase alone explains why the cotton industry grew?

2 The supply of raw cotton became much more plentiful, which meant that the finished product was cheaper and more people could afford it. When America was a British colony the growing of cotton was banned in order to protect Britain's trade with her colonies in the West Indies and India. However, America became independent in 1783 and the Americans looked for new products to grow and sell. Cotton plantations soon became very successful in the southern states of America and imports of raw cotton from the USA into Britain grew from under £500,000 in 1790 to £55 million by 1810. This development in the cotton trade led Britain into the modern industrialised world.

3 People spent more money in the eighteenth century, some of which was spent on clothes. This is similar to our first reason in that it suggests that there was an increase in demand for cotton.

4 There was a great expansion in trade. Britain was the world's leading trading nation in the late eighteenth century. British ships carrying goods could be found all over the world. This meant that cotton manufacturers were not limited to the amount of cotton they could sell at home – there was a huge export market. By the early nineteenth century cotton goods made up nearly half of all British exports. Woollen cloth and raw wool also became valuable exports as the northern wool towns became world famous for the high quality of their products.

New inventions

A series of new inventions speeded up the process of making cotton goods. These were the most important new textile machines:

DATE	MACHINE	INVENTOR	RESULT
These machines could be used at home:			
1733	Flying Shuttle	John Kay	Made weaving into a much quicker process.
1764	The Spinning Jenny	James Hargreaves	Could spin eight yarns at once.
These machines were big and needed factories:			
1769	The Water Frame	Richard Arkwright	Powered by water and therefore could only be used in factories. Made much stronger thread.
1784	The Mule	Samuel Crompton	Made high-quality strong thread.
1786	The Power Loom	Edmund Cartwright	Continued to be adapted until it slowly took over weaving. Powered by water or steam.

• Which machines were for spinning and which were for weaving? Why do you think that an improvement in weaving was likely to lead to an improvement in spinning?

18

WATER FRAME

SPINNING JENNY

POWER LOOM

SPINNING MULES IN A FACTORY

SPINNING MULE

Richard Arkwright – father of the factory system?

Historians have argued about how Britain was able to become the first industrial nation. One of the things they have disagreed about is how much importance to attach to the individual inventors. You can see from the table of inventions that Richard Arkwright was responsible for the introduction of a factory machine called the Water Frame.

Some of the early inventors such as James Hargreaves had their ideas stolen and made no money out of their inventions. Arkwright was determined to be different. He was a barber by trade, but travelling in Lancashire he knew that there was a huge demand for cheap yarn and he decided to do something about this.

Source D

A portrait of Richard Arkwright.

Source E

'In 1767, Arkwright met Kay, the clockmaker, at Warrington. He persuaded Kay to go with him first to Preston and afterwards to Nottingham. It is true that Arkwright had been experimenting in mechanics, but there is no evidence to show that he had ever thought of making a spinning machine before his interview with Kay.'

Edward Baines, *History of the Cotton Manufacturer in Great Britain*, 1835

Arkwright needed financial help if his invention was to make money. He found a partner, Jedediah Strutt, a hosiery manufacturer. His backing meant that he could try to improve his machine and build several factories, the first of which was at Cromford in Derbyshire. He was also the first to use steam power in a cotton mill. His workers had to work 12-hour shifts to boost his profits.

Source F

'Mr Arkwright was not the inventor. His so-called "great mechanical abilities" consisted solely in having cunning enough to pump a secret out of a silly talkative clockmaker, and having sense enough to know when he saw a good invention.'

Richard Guest, *A History of the Cotton Manufacturers*, 1823

● What point are these two writers trying to make about Arkwright?

1 Imagine that you are a professional historian. A modern textile firm has asked you to produce a leaflet explaining to the public how Britain's cotton factories led the world. You should mention: the population increase; the supply of raw cotton; increased spending; new inventions.

2 a What part did Richard Arkwright play in developing the cotton industry?
b How many reasons can you find to explain why Arkwright was so successful?

4 Iron, coal and steam

The first factories were powered by running water and their machines were largely wooden. The coming of cheap iron and steam power changed this and led to an explosion of new factories and new industries.

How was industry changed by the use of iron and steam power?

A problem for the iron masters

The wealth of Britain in the nineteenth century depended on machines made of iron and driven by steam engines. Although iron had been made for many thousands of years, iron manufacturers had great problems in the early eighteenth century. They used charcoal to heat iron ore in a furnace, but a growing shortage of wood made charcoal very expensive.

Developments in the iron industry

In 1709 Abraham Darby of Coalbrookdale in Shropshire made a great breakthrough. He found a way of using coke, which is made from coal, to smelt the iron. Darby's discovery was limited to the making of brittle *cast-iron* – good enough for cooking pots but not for machinery. To make cast-iron, molten iron is simply poured into a mould. Better-quality *wrought-iron* requires further work to remove impurities. At this time wrought-iron was made in small charcoal-burning forges; here iron was reheated and hammered into more flexible wrought-iron. In 1784 Henry Cort invented a new method of making wrought-iron in a huge coal-fired furnace – by stirring the molten iron and pushing it through enormous rollers. This led to an enormous increase in the production of good-quality wrought-iron.

The railways and machinery of the first half of the nineteenth century were made from iron. In the latter part of the century, steel began to take over as the basic material of industry. Steel is made by mixing wrought-iron with carbon. Although it had been discovered many centuries before, it remained too expensive for widespread use until Henry Bessemer invented a better way of making steel in 1856. Bessemer's invention was a container called a 'converter' which could make steel quickly and cheaply.

Source A *A Bessemer converter.*

21

The coming of steam

Steam engines use coal to heat water and create steam. The pressure of the steam is used to turn a piston. Simple steam engines had been used as pumps in mines since 1712. In 1766 a Scottish engineer, James Watt, made dramatic improvements in the design of steam engines so that they would be more powerful and burn less coal. In 1781 Watt found a way of getting a steam engine to turn a wheel; steam engines could now be used in the early factories instead of water wheels. Over the next hundred years steam provided the power for more and more industries.

Source B

Watt's double-acting condensing steam engine.

Source C

The invention of steam power led to the development of new machines such as James Naysmyth's steam hammer.

Source D

'Steam engines create a vast demand for fuel and they call into employment multitudes of miners, engineers, shipbuilders and sailors, and cause the construction of canals and railways.'

Andrew Ure, *The Philosophy of Manufacture*, 1835

Source E

An early mine in south Wales.

Effects on the population

The rise of steam and coal brought about a shift in the geography of Britain. For many centuries the most prosperous part of Britain had been the south-east of England. Reliance on coal brought new wealth to the north and west of Britain. New communities developed, for example, in the coal-rich valleys of south Wales. Much of the Welsh coal was shipped from the port of Cardiff and the population of Cardiff rose from 2,000 in 1800 to 164,000 in 1900. The demand for coal and iron led to thousands of new jobs in the western Lowlands of Scotland; this was the reason behind a rise in the population of Glasgow from 77,000 in 1800 to 904,000 by 1900.

These boom towns of the nineteenth century faced many problems in the twentieth century when the age of steam and coal came to an end.

Source F

The Iron Forge *by Joseph Wright, 1772*.

---

1 How did Abraham Darby improve the production of cast-iron?

2 How did Henry Cort change the way wrought-iron was made?

3 Why was coal important to both Darby and Cort?

4 How did steam engines change British industry?

24

5 Canals, roads and railways

As more goods were produced there was a growing need for better transport to move products to the places where people wanted to buy them. Farmers, factory owners and merchants all needed better services. In the early eighteenth century most roads were poor and water transport was slow and inconvenient. However, by 1900 Britain could claim to have one of the most efficient transport systems in the world. There were two distinct phases to this change: 1750–1830: the age of canals and turnpikes; 1830–1900: the age of railways.

How was a new transport system created?

Canal mania

The new factories depended on coal. It was coal that fuelled steam engines and iron foundries. Businessmen needed to find a way to move coal across the country and they found the answer in new canals. The great expansion of canals started in the 1760s but the history of canals goes back much further than this. For many centuries merchants had used barges on rivers to move their goods. Between 1650 and 1750 much effort was put into improving these waterways. It was a small step from digging new channels for rivers to making completely new canals.

The first significant canal in the British Isles was the Newry Canal built in 1742 in Ireland. It was 35 miles long and carried coal to Dublin. Great excitement was caused in 1761 when the Bridgewater Canal opened in Lancashire.

The eighth wonder of the world

The Duke of Bridgewater owned coal mines on his Lancashire estate, but he had no means of getting his coal to Manchester quickly and cheaply. Eventually he solved the problem by building a canal. His engineer was called James Brindley. When the canal was opened people were amazed by the daring aqueduct Brindley built to carry the coal over a river. As soon as the canal was in operation the price of coal in Manchester immediately halved.

Bridgewater made a great deal of money from his canal and other people decided to copy him. By the 1790s a national network of canals had been created so that cargo could cross the country from Liverpool to London. Between 1758 and 1802, 165 canals were created to carry heavy cargoes like coal.

Source A
The Barton Aqueduct on the Bridgewater Canal, 1761.

Source B

A passenger coach, about 1830.

Source C
The Railway Station *by William Powell-Frith.*

The turnpike trusts
Light freight, post and passengers continued to go by road because it remained quicker. Many of Britain's roads had not been rebuilt or improved since Roman times. As industry grew, attempts were made to build better roads for the increased traffic. In the eighteenth century there was therefore an increase in *turnpike trust*s set up by groups of landowners and merchants. The trust was responsible for all repairs and improvements in a section of road. Parliament gave the trust permission to charge all travellers who used that section.

Faster journeys
However, it was not only the quality of the roads which led to a reduction in journey time. In the eighteenth century the quickest form of travel was the stage coach. By 1800 these coaches were a great deal better than those of a century earlier. Improvements such as narrower wheels had increased their speed. From the 1780s coaches began to be used to carry letters. Before this, letters were carried by postboys on horseback. This table shows you how the road and vehicle improvements were able to change travelling times by coach between London and Manchester.

Year	Journey time
1700	98 hours or more
1760	48 hours
1830	19 hours

Improved road transport helped many merchants and manufacturers to get their goods to customers safely and more quickly, but it was not a solution for transporting heavy goods.

The coming of the railway

While transport improved dramatically between 1750 and 1830 some problems remained. Road transport was poor for carrying heavy goods. Canals were slow: it took 36 hours to move cotton by barge the few miles from Liverpool to Manchester. The use of steam-driven engines on iron tracks changed all this. Railway trains were both fast and capable of carrying heavy goods.

The idea of carts on tracks or tram-ways was not new: horse-powered railways were widely used before 1800 for quarrying and mining. In the years after 1800 there was great rivalry between engineers to see who could design a steam engine able to pull carriages. In 1804 a Cornishman, Richard Trevithick, built a locomotive that could pull freight by rail at Merthyr Tydfil in south Wales. The world's first public steam railway, engineered by George Stephenson, was opened in 1825 and ran between Stockton and Darlington. But the great breakthrough to the railway age came in 1830 when a railway was opened between Liverpool and Manchester to carry both goods and passengers. The engine which pulled the train was the famous *Rocket* designed by Stephenson.

What was the effect of the railways?

Railway building took place on a massive scale after 1830. In 1832, 166 miles of track were open. By 1850 there were 6,559 miles of railway in use. Unlike the canals the railways provided good transport for passengers. In 1836 it took a traveller thirty hours to get from Newcastle to London by road. By 1844 the train journey took only twelve hours. The building of the railways was a great boost to industry because of the huge amount of iron that was required. Once in operation, railways helped businesses to move raw materials and goods much more effectively. Not surprisingly, many canals soon lost most of their customers.

GEO. STEPHENSON'S ROCKET, 1829.

Source D
Stephenson's Rocket.

The development of the railways was dominated by the engineering genius of Isambard Kingdom Brunel. When he was only 27 years of age, Brunel became chief engineer to the Great Western Railway. Between 1835 and 1841 he built the line from London to Bristol, which was considered to be the finest piece of railway engineering of the time.

Source E
The dramatic consequences of the railway were commented upon by people at the time. This was written only two years after the railway opened:

'Before the railway there were twenty-nine coaches which could carry 688 people each day. The railway has carried an average of 1,070 people a day. The fare for the railway is half of that of the coach. The journey by coach had taken four hours. By railway it is one hour and three quarters. Only one coach is still running. Goods are delivered the same day. By canal it took three days. It has saved the Manchester Cotton Manufacturers at least £20,000 a year.'

The Annual Register, 1832

Source F
Isambard Kingdom Brunel.

Social consequences of transport changes

The needs of industry were the driving force behind the rapid transport changes, but the consequences of the improvements went beyond this. For example, improved road travel led to more newspapers being widely available and to the growth of coaching inns. The railways in particular had many important social consequences.

The middle classes and some working-class people used the railways to get away from the towns to the countryside and seaside. It was not only the basic necessities like cheap food which were carried by the railways: newspapers were transported by rail, and music-hall performers and touring theatrical companies were able to travel around the country by train. After the coming of the railways Britain was a more closely knit community in which life moved at a faster pace than had previously been possible.

Source G

This map shows the railways which had been built by 1852.
After 1830 the railway network in Britain grew so rapidly that within twenty years most of the industrial areas were served with transport.

---

1 Make a time chart to show important changes in transport between 1700 and 1900.

2 Explain in your own words why canals and turnpike roads made transport better.

3 Why was the steam engine vital to the development of the railway?

4 How did railways develop between 1804 and 1850?

5 What were the results of the growth of the railways?

6 A worldwide Empire

In 1750 Britain already possessed some colonies overseas. This was land which had been settled and was governed by British people. By 1900 this had grown to a vast Empire with one-fifth of the world's land under British control.

Why did Britain's Empire expand? What was its impact upon British society?

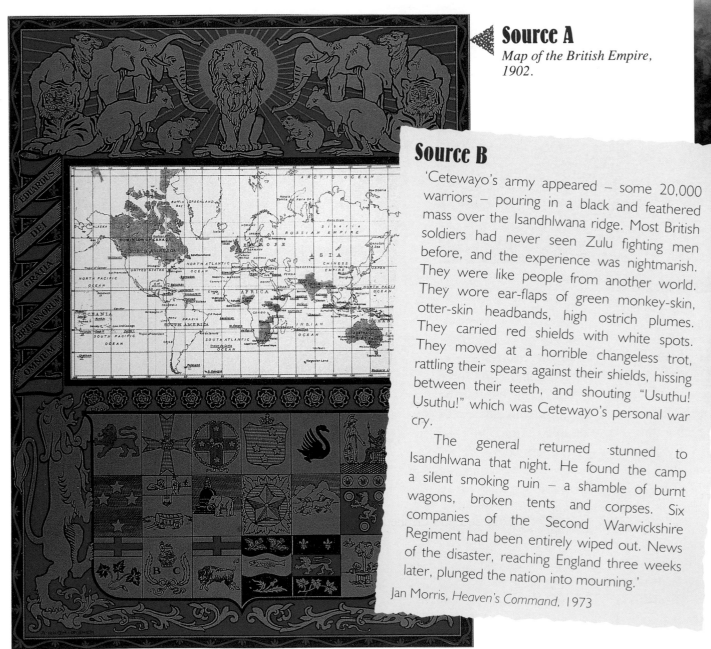

Source A
Map of the British Empire, 1902.

Source B

'Cetewayo's army appeared – some 20,000 warriors – pouring in a black and feathered mass over the Isandhlwana ridge. Most British soldiers had never seen Zulu fighting men before, and the experience was nightmarish. They were like people from another world. They wore ear-flaps of green monkey-skin, otter-skin headbands, high ostrich plumes. They carried red shields with white spots. They moved at a horrible changeless trot, rattling their spears against their shields, hissing between their teeth, and shouting "Usuthu! Usuthu!" which was Cetewayo's personal war cry.

The general returned stunned to Isandhlwana that night. He found the camp a silent smoking ruin – a shamble of burnt wagons, broken tents and corpses. Six companies of the Second Warwickshire Regiment had been entirely wiped out. News of the disaster, reaching England three weeks later, plunged the nation into mourning.'

Jan Morris, *Heaven's Command*, 1973

War with the Zulus
In January 1879 British troops invaded Zululand. In Source B a modern British writer describes what happened when Zulu warriors, led by their king, Cetewayo, took the British troops by surprise.

● What impression does the writer give us of the Zulu people? What are the strengths and weaknesses of this extract as a way of writing history?

Source C

The Battle of Isandhlwana, 1879 *painted by
Charles Edwin Fripp.*

- *How does the painting make you feel about the British
soldiers and the Zulu warriors?*

  Why do you think the artist painted this picture?

The growth of the Empire

To understand why British and Zulu soldiers clashed
in 1879 we need to understand the way the British
Empire grew.

British colonies abroad date back to the sixteenth
and seventeenth centuries. In the Caribbean, Britain
controlled Jamaica, Barbados and some smaller
islands. These Caribbean islands were very valuable
as the base for the money-spinning sugar industry.
Between 1756 and 1763 Britain fought a war with
France for control of foreign territories. Britain won,

and this meant that India and what we now call
Canada would be British and not French colonies.

The British Empire continued to grow during this
period. The Australian colony of New South Wales
was established in 1788. In the Caribbean, Trinidad
and Tobago were added to the British possessions.
Starting with Cape Colony in 1806 a whole series of
territories were seized in Africa. In the Far East the
British took control of Singapore in 1819 and Hong
Kong in 1842.

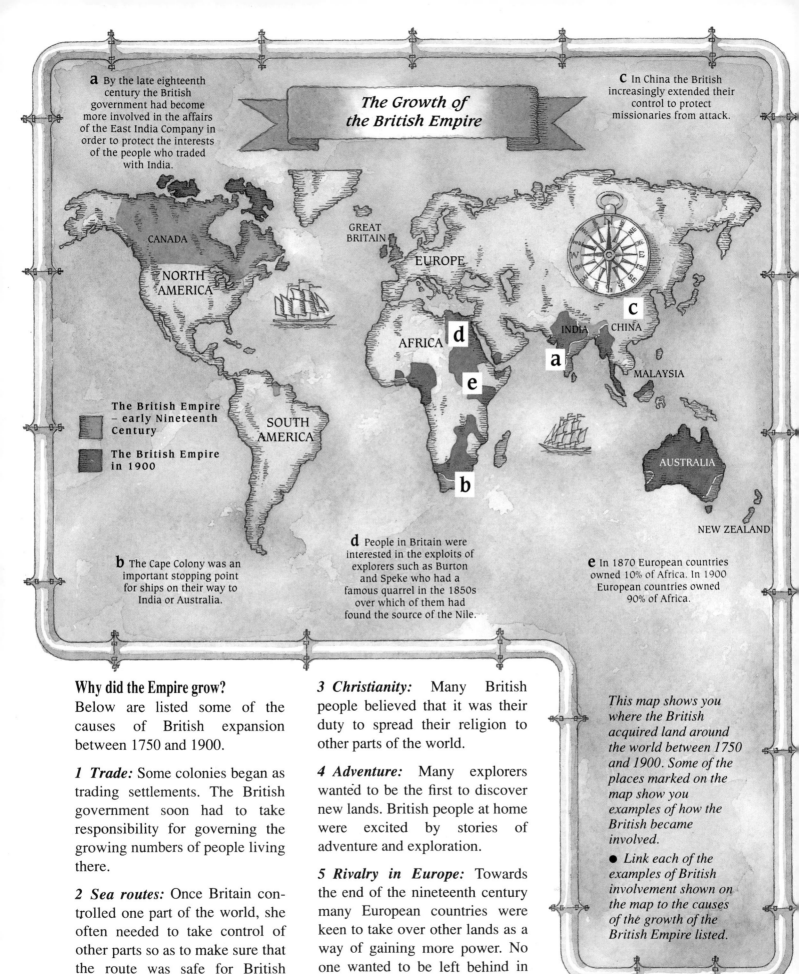

a By the late eighteenth century the British government had become more involved in the affairs of the East India Company in order to protect the interests of the people who traded with India.

c In China the British increasingly extended their control to protect missionaries from attack.

The Growth of the British Empire

CANADA

NORTH AMERICA

GREAT BRITAIN

EUROPE

AFRICA

d

a

INDIA

CHINA

c

MALAYSIA

e

The British Empire – early Nineteenth Century

The British Empire in 1900

SOUTH AMERICA

b

AUSTRALIA

NEW ZEALAND

b The Cape Colony was an important stopping point for ships on their way to India or Australia.

d People in Britain were interested in the exploits of explorers such as Burton and Speke who had a famous quarrel in the 1850s over which of them had found the source of the Nile.

e In 1870 European countries owned 10% of Africa. In 1900 European countries owned 90% of Africa.

Why did the Empire grow?

Below are listed some of the causes of British expansion between 1750 and 1900.

1 Trade: Some colonies began as trading settlements. The British government soon had to take responsibility for governing the growing numbers of people living there.

2 Sea routes: Once Britain controlled one part of the world, she often needed to take control of other parts so as to make sure that the route was safe for British ships.

3 Christianity: Many British people believed that it was their duty to spread their religion to other parts of the world.

4 Adventure: Many explorers wanted to be the first to discover new lands. British people at home were excited by stories of adventure and exploration.

5 Rivalry in Europe: Towards the end of the nineteenth century many European countries were keen to take over other lands as a way of gaining more power. No one wanted to be left behind in the race for new territory.

This map shows you where the British acquired land around the world between 1750 and 1900. Some of the places marked on the map show you examples of how the British became involved.

● *Link each of the examples of British involvement shown on the map to the causes of the growth of the British Empire listed.*

Effects of the Empire

What were the consequences of the Empire for British people at home? Each of the following sources reveals something about these effects.

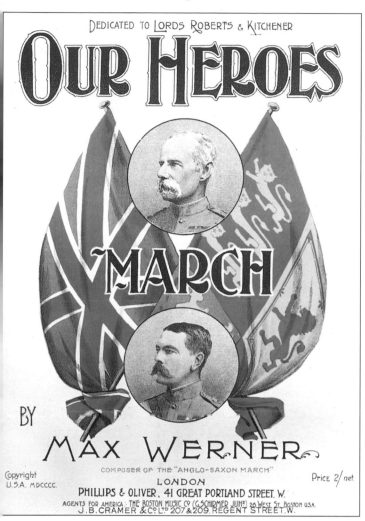

Disraeli, one of Britain's Prime Ministers in the nineteenth century, used the Empire as a way of gaining votes. He said he wanted Britain to be 'a great country, a country where your sons rise to the highest positions, and obtain not only the respect of fellow countrymen, but command the respect of the entire world'.

● *How did Disraeli want the rest of the world to feel about Britain?*

Source D

Sheet music was very widely used in the days before radio and television. This was the cover of a popular piece of sheet music. Make some suggestions as to what Roberts and Kitchener might have done to be regarded as heroes.

Source G — William Gladstone

Source E

Many people saw the main role of the army as keeping peace, not making war. Lord Randolph Churchill, speaking to the Primrose League in 1885 on his return from India, where about one-third of the British army was stationed, said that British rule was 'a sheet of oil spread over the surface of an immense and deep ocean of people, keeping it calm and quiet and unruffled by storms'.

Another British Prime Minister, Gladstone, opposed the expansion of the Empire. He wrote about the war with the Zulus: 'In Africa 10,000 Zulus had been slaughtered for no other offence than their attempt to defend with their naked bodies, their hearths and homes, their wives and families, against your artillery.'

33

Source H ▶

This nineteenth-century cartoon is an example of the popular view of Britain's kindness to the less fortunate of the world.

● *Which country does the man represent? What is the baby on the doorstep meant to be?*

Source I ▼

Queen Victoria presenting a Bible *by Thomas Jones Barker, 1861. The Queen became a symbol in Britain and throughout the colonies of the triumph of the Empire.*

● *What impression has the artist created of the relationship between Britain and the people in the rest of the Empire?*

THE BLACK BABY.

---

1 How and why did the British Empire grow between 1750 and 1900?

2 Here is a list of various effects of the Empire. The sources in this unit tell us something about these effects. Match up one or more of the sources with each effect.
The Empire:
◆ created popular heroes
◆ made the Queen more popular
◆ created opportunities for celebration
◆ encouraged the belief that the British were a superior race
◆ extended knowledge and curiosity about the rest of the world

3 a Taking all these effects together, what impression do they create of the British Empire at this time?
b Look back at the causes of the growth of the British Empire on page 32. Do the reasons for the expansion create a different impression to the effects listed in sources D – I?

7 A trading nation

In the eighteenth and nineteenth centuries Britain's trade expanded in a number of ways. The amount of goods imported and exported increased, the distances across which trade took place became much greater, and the range of goods that Britain was trading in became much wider. Of course, these changes did not occur steadily and evenly. There were times of rapid increase and times of slower increase and even decline.

How did the expansion of trade affect Britain?

Source A

This picture shows the docks in eighteenth-century Bristol.

● *What signs are there in the picture that Bristol people were involved in trade? What kinds of work was this creating?*

The growth of factories in Britain was closely connected with trade. Britain sold many of its factory-made goods abroad and bought raw materials, such as raw cotton, from other countries. In 1750 Britain had long been a trading country with a large merchant navy and important ports. There was an established system of finance and insurance for people who wanted to organise trading voyages.

Source B

'The Liverpool merchants trade round the whole island, send ships to Norway, to Hamburg and to the Baltic, as also to Holland and Flanders. In a word, they are almost become like the Londoners – universal merchants. They import almost all kinds of foreign goods, they have consequently a great inland trade. There is no town in England, London excepted, that can equal Liverpool for the fineness of the streets and beauty of the buildings.'

Daniel Defoe, *A Tour through the Whole Island of Great Britain,* 1726

Trade expands

These are three important economic developments that took place in the eighteenth century:

Some people grew much richer.

There was a growing population.

Britain had close ties with its worldwide Empire.

● Explain carefully how you think each of these would lead to a growth in trade.

Trade increased during the eighteenth century with a great upsurge in the last years of the century dominated by the increase in the export of textiles. Britain fought a disastrous war with the new United States of America between 1775 and 1783 and, as you can see from Source C, this led to a temporary fall in the growth of trade. But figures like these do not tell the full story – a large amount of trade was undertaken secretly by smuggling and this particularly affected imports of luxury silks and brandy from France.

Growth of overseas trade

Sources D and E show you which parts of the world Britain was trading with.

Source C – England's overseas trade

	Exports £ million	Imports £ million
1740	8.2	6.7
1750	12.7	7.8
1760	14.7	9.8
1770	14.3	12.2
1780	12.5	10.8
1790	18.9	17.4

Source D – Britain's world trade routes in 1740

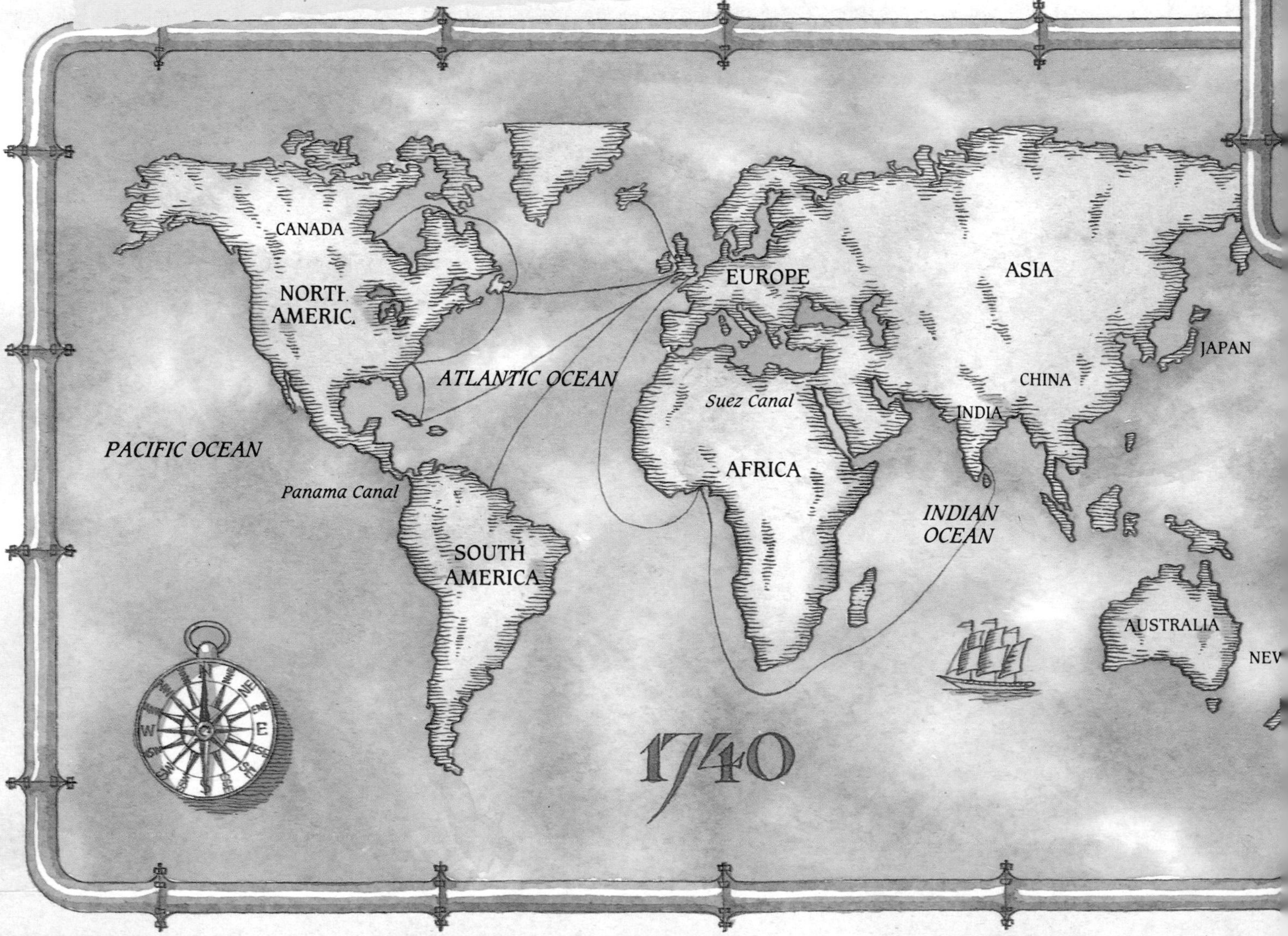

CANADA

NORTH AMERICA

EUROPE

ASIA

JAPAN

CHINA

ATLANTIC OCEAN

Suez Canal

INDIA

PACIFIC OCEAN

Panama Canal

AFRICA

INDIAN OCEAN

SOUTH AMERICA

AUSTRALIA

NEW

1740

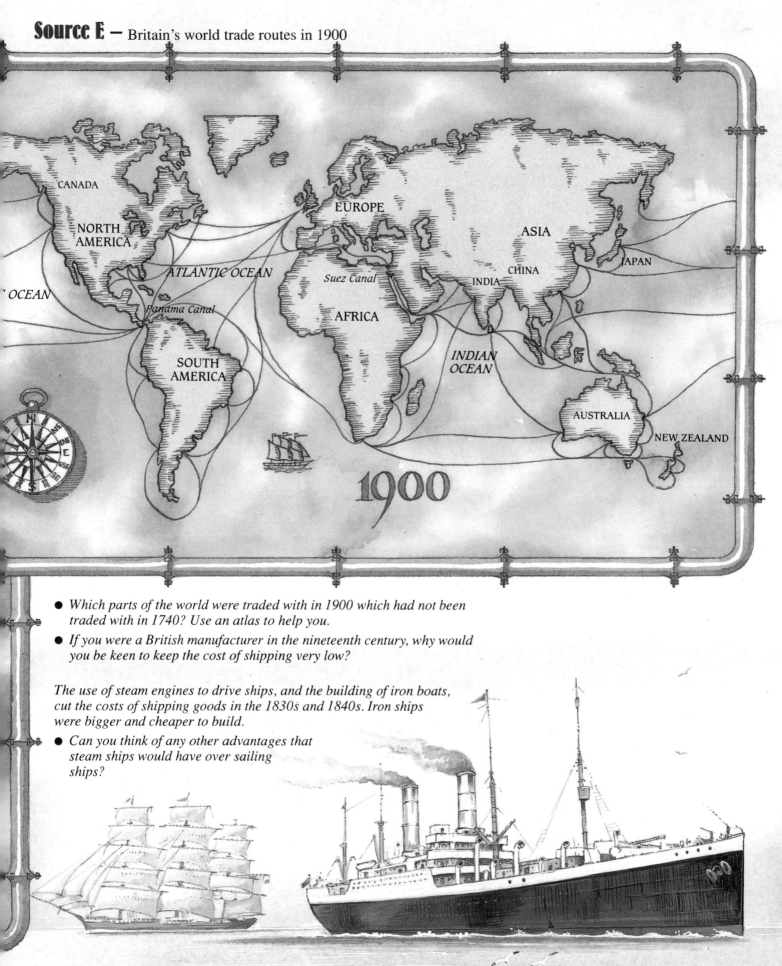

- *Which parts of the world were traded with in 1900 which had not been traded with in 1740? Use an atlas to help you.*

- *If you were a British manufacturer in the nineteenth century, why would you be keen to keep the cost of shipping very low?*

The use of steam engines to drive ships, and the building of iron boats, cut the costs of shipping goods in the 1830s and 1840s. Iron ships were bigger and cheaper to build.

- *Can you think of any other advantages that steam ships would have over sailing ships?*

The slave trade

One aspect of trade in the eighteenth century was very different from the rest. British merchants bought slaves in West Africa and shipped them across the Atlantic to sell them in America and especially the Caribbean. Between 1700 and 1810 British ships transported over 3,000,000 African slaves. The trade came to a climax in the 1780s when British traders shipped nearly 50,000 people every year. The ports of London, Bristol and Liverpool were the base for the slave ships. After the 1740s, Liverpool came to dominate the slave trade, and by 1800 Liverpool ships carried over 75% of all the British trade.

Source F

Slavers on the Guinea Coast
by A. F. Biard.

A three-way trade

The merchants of Liverpool and other ports bought slaves in West Africa in exchange for British textiles, iron goods and other manufactured items. To pay for the slaves the landowners in the Caribbean sent great amounts of sugar back to Britain. The slaves themselves were forced to work on the sugar plantations. Although historians disagree about the details there seems to be little doubt that the slave trade made Britain a richer country and this meant that more money was available to spend at home.

Source G

'The planters do not want to be told that their Negroes are human creatures. If they believe them to be of human kind they cannot think of them as dogs or horses.'

Edward Long, 1774

Source H

A Scottish lawyer and writer thought slavery was right:

'God has approved of slavery and to abolish it would be robbery. Ending slavery would be extreme cruelty to the African savages, who are made much happier by it.'

James Boswell

Attitudes to slavery

In 1750 many educated people approved of slavery. Slave traders were respected members of society. How could people justify the horrific business of slavery?

Attitudes to slavery began to change between 1750 and 1800. A small number of Christians led a campaign against slavery. In 1772 a judge declared that no one could be kept as a slave in England. Opponents of the slave trade found a friend in the Member of Parliament, William Wilberforce. Wilberforce and others persuaded the government to abolish the British slave trade in 1807. Wilberforce then turned his attention to the existence of slavery in the British Empire; it was finally banned in 1833.

Trade and government

Opinions on the role of government in organising trade changed during this period.

On the map:

NORTH AMERICA

BRITAIN

ATLANTIC OCEAN

Sugar, rum, tobacco, cotton - bought with money from selling slaves

Brandy, cloth, iron goods - traded for slaves

WEST INDIES

WEST AFRICA

Slaves "Middle Passage" 2 months voyage

SOUTH AMERICA

Protectionism

In the eighteenth century a system of protecting industry and controlling trade meant that only Britain could trade with British colonies. The government also placed customs duties on goods coming into Britain from abroad to encourage people to buy British goods.

Free trade

By the 1770s some economists began to say that restrictions on trade were wrong. In 1776 Adam Smith published a book called *The Wealth of Nations*. In it he argued for 'free trade'. This meant reducing or abolishing customs duties which he believed hindered trade. Goods would be cheap and increased trade would bring wealth and wages. These views were increasingly accepted by the government and from the 1820s duties began to be lowered. In 1842 the value of British exports was £47,250,000. By 1870 they were worth £200,000,000. Not surprisingly, British businessmen were increasingly confident that free trade was good for their industries.

The struggle over the Corn Law

Disagreements about protection and free trade became very bitter in the first half of the nineteenth century. Landlords and farmers were keen on protection because they wanted to keep the price of food high so that they could keep up their profits. Parliament was keen to please these people and passed a Corn Law in 1815 restricting the importation of wheat. This divided the country; people in the new factory towns around Manchester thought it was wrong.

Eventually they set up an organisation called the Anti Corn Law League to fight for free trade in food. In 1846 the Prime Minister, Robert Peel, gave in to the free trade arguments and scrapped the Corn Law.

---

1 Look at Source C. How can we tell from this that Britain was a great trading nation even before 1750?

2 Why did trade expand in the eighteenth century? What was the most important item that was exported in the late eighteenth century?

3 How was the slave trade organised?

4 Today most people think that slavery is wicked. Why did some educated people believe in slavery in the eighteenth century?

5 a Explain in your own words the difference between free trade and protectionism.
b Produce a poster for the Anti Corn Law League in 1845. Make it clear why you think taxing imported food is wrong.

CHANGES IN SOCIETY

The new mines and mills depended on men, women and children working long hours, often in dangerous conditions for low wages. Accidents were common and the maimed child or adult would be dismissed to become a beggar or an inmate of a workhouse.

Workers joined together forming trade unions to get better wages and conditions from their employers. Early unions were not very successful and were strictly controlled by government laws. It was not until the mid nineteenth century that unions established themselves.

As towns and cities grew in size, life could be very grim for the poor as living conditions could be appalling. Diseases like cholera spread because of overcrowding and poor sanitation. During this period the rich built impressive public buildings and splendid homes in which they lived comfortably.

Between 1750 and 1900 the Anglican Church became less important in Britain. There was an apparent decline in religious belief, and new scientific thinking challenged religion. But there was also a growing religious movement called Methodism, which became very popular in Wales, Cornwall and the new industrial towns.

During the nineteenth century about 12 million people left Britain to begin new lives in various parts of the British Empire and the USA. Most left because of economic hardship. Smaller groups of people came to Britain escaping from famine and persecution in other countries but they often lived in poor conditions and were sometimes badly treated once they arrived.

Women had very few rights during this period although they played an important part in the economy of the country. They were banned from most well-paid jobs and very few were educated. Some improvements were made in the second half of the nineteenth century but women still did not have the right to vote by 1900.

Before 1830 the government provided virtually no education and it was not until 1880 that all children had to attend school until they were ten years old. Conditions gradually improved throughout the nineteenth century with more children being provided with a balanced education. Nevertheless, many children still lived in conditions of extreme poverty and were treated very harshly.

Work for many people in the period 1750–1900 was a brutal experience. Some artists disturbed people with the pictures they produced showing the actual lives of working people. Other artists of the period can be criticised for the false or unreal impression they created of the lives of working people.

8 Child labour in mills and mines

The new factories and mines depended on the work of children. Conditions in these places of work were often appalling. At first, child workers had little protection provided by the government.

What was life like for children at work?

Working at a young age

The first factories were full of children. At the time there was no education for most children and it was expected that by the age of seven, children should be at work. In the fields and workshops that existed before the factories children worked as part of family groups of workers, and this lived on in the new places of work. Parents saw it as natural that their children should be bringing in a wage at the earliest possible age. Factory owners valued child labour because children were paid less and were often more nimble and skilful than their parents.

Life in the mill

Sources A and B show men, women and children at work in mills in the first half of the nineteenth century.

Source A

Children working in a factory in the early nineteenth century.

● *What do you think the child on the floor is doing?*

Source C

This is taken from an interview with Gillett Sharpe, who lived in Keighley in Yorkshire:

'My boy, Edwin, was well known for being lively and straight before he went to the mill, but after three years he was weak in his knees and it was so bad that he could hardly walk. Many people told me to take him away but I was a poor man with a large family and needed his wages.'

Parliamentary Report, 1831–32

● Why do you think that Edwin Sharpe was no longer 'lively and straight' after three years of work in the mill? Use all the evidence in the unit so far.

Source B

Mill workers, 1830.

● *How do both of these pictures suggest that it might have been dangerous working in these early factories? What are the other similarities between these two pictures? In what ways do the two pictures give very different impressions of factory life?*

Working conditions

Conditions in the factories varied. At worst, children were subjected to merciless cruelty. Working conditions were extremely dangerous and in the early 1830s parliament investigated. The different investigations by parliament produced hundreds of accounts of hardship. Sources C and D are two examples of these. The investigations found that very long hours of work, accidents, ill-health and the beating of children were all common.

Source D

Samuel Coulson's daughters worked up to 18 hours a day. This is how he found the eldest girl once when returning to his home in Leeds:

'I saw her shoulders and asked her what the matter was. She said, "The overlooker has strapped me, but do not complain for we will be sacked." The overlooker had strapped her because she hadn't done as she was told immediately. Her back was beat nearly to a jelly and you could see the marks even a fortnight later.'

Parliamentary Report, 1831–32

● If Samuel Coulson's daughter worked eighteen hours a day, why might this have prevented her from doing as she was told immediately?

Down the pit

Extremely harsh conditions were experienced by the men, women and children who worked in the mines. Women and children usually worked only in the smaller, more old-fashioned pits. This picture shows you the kinds of work which would have been done underground.

Source E

A woman and child working in a mine.

A modern illustrator's impression of an explosion in a mine caused by 'firedamp' – an accumulation of gases igniting.

44

Sources E–H give us a picture of some of the worst conditions in the mines in the last half of the nineteenth century. Read the sources and compare the conditions with those in the mills.

Source F – The Collier Lass

Songs like this were used to express the experience of ordinary working people:

'My name's Polly Parker, I come o'er from Worsley
My father and brother work in the coal mine.
Our family's large, we have got seven children,
So I am obliged to work in the same mine.
As this is my fortune, I know you'll feel sorry,
That in such employment my days shall pass.
I keep up my spirits, I sing and look merry,
Although I am but a poor collier lass.

By the greatest of dangers each day I'm surrounded;
I hang in the air by a rope or a chain.
The mine may fall in, I may be killed or wounded,
May perish by damp or the fire of the train.
And what would you do if it weren't for our labour?
In wretched starvation your days you would pass,
While we could provide you with life's greatest blessing
Then do not despise the poor collier lass.'

Source G

This is an extract from an interview with Patience Kershaw, aged 17, which took place during parliament's investigation in 1842:

'I push tubs of coal. The bald place on my head is made by thrusting the tubs. I push the tubs a mile and more underground and back; they weigh three hundredweight; I push eleven a day. The coal-diggers that I work for beat me with their hands if I am not quick enough. I am the only girl in the pit. There are about twenty boys and fifteen men. All the men are naked. I would rather work in the mill than in the coal-pit.'

Parliamentary Report, 1842

Source H

This is an extract from the same report, describing the work of the youngest children:

'They are called "trappers". They sit in a little hole and open and shut the doors. They are in the pit the whole time it is worked, frequently about twelve hours a day. They sit in the dark, often with a damp floor. Their ages vary from five to ten years.'

An alternative view

The parliamentary reports on working conditions shocked many people. However, others argued that there was nothing wrong with children working in factories or mines and that it was up to the parents to decide whether to send their children out to work. Factory owners saw child labour as absolutely necessary. As for reports of cruelty or damage to health, many said that these were greatly exaggerated.

Source I

The Marquess of Londonderry owned many pits in the north-east of England. He presented a petition in 1842 to the House of Lords, protesting at the 1842 inquiry:

'The trapper's job is neither cheerless nor dull; nor is he kept alone and in darkness all the time. The trapper is generally cheerful and contented.'

House of Lords Debates, 24 June 1842

● Why is it possible that the Marquess of Londonderry is exaggerating the happiness of the trapper children?

Source J

Andrew Ure was a doctor and a keen supporter of the new industries:

'I have visited many factories during a period of several months and I never saw a single beating of a child, nor indeed did I see children unhappy. They seemed to be cheerful and alert, taking pleasure in the gentle use of their muscles. The work of these lively elves seemed to me to be like a sport. They showed no signs of being exhausted.'

Andrew Ure, *The Philosophy of Manufacture*, 1835

Sources I and J may not give us the whole truth, but it is possible that some of the sources earlier in the unit do not give the whole truth either. It is likely that conditions were extremely bad in many places of work, but some of the people commenting upon these conditions might also have been exaggerating.

● Why do you think they might have done this?

The Factory Acts

The government started to take an interest in factory conditions at the start of the nineteenth century. Laws were passed in 1802 and 1819 to reduce the hours of work for some children in cotton mills but they made little difference because no one enforced the laws.

In the 1820s a strong campaign began to restrict the use of child labour. One of its leaders, Richard Oastler, wrote a powerful series of letters suggesting that child workers were little more than slaves. This campaign led the government to further action. The table opposite describes the important laws on factory work that the government introduced.

A problem solved?

If we only look at the laws passed by parliament we do not get the full picture of how much change took place. Historians need to ask how effective the Factory Acts were and also how many other serious problems were not touched by them. There was, to some extent, a hidden picture behind the reforms.

Problems with inspection

Even after the Factory Acts were passed, some employers continued to cheat and break the laws. There were not enough inspectors and fines were so low that an employer might think that they were worth risking. Also, in some areas of the new laws it was extremely difficult to tell if a factory owner was breaking the law.

● Which would be the harder to enforce, a law about fencing dangerous machinery or a law limiting the hours a 9-year-old worked?

Smaller workplaces

Only about half of all industrial workers worked in large workplaces which could be described as factories. Smaller workshops were not included in the laws until 1867. Even then many kinds of worker would still have been unaffected by the new laws limiting hours of work.

46

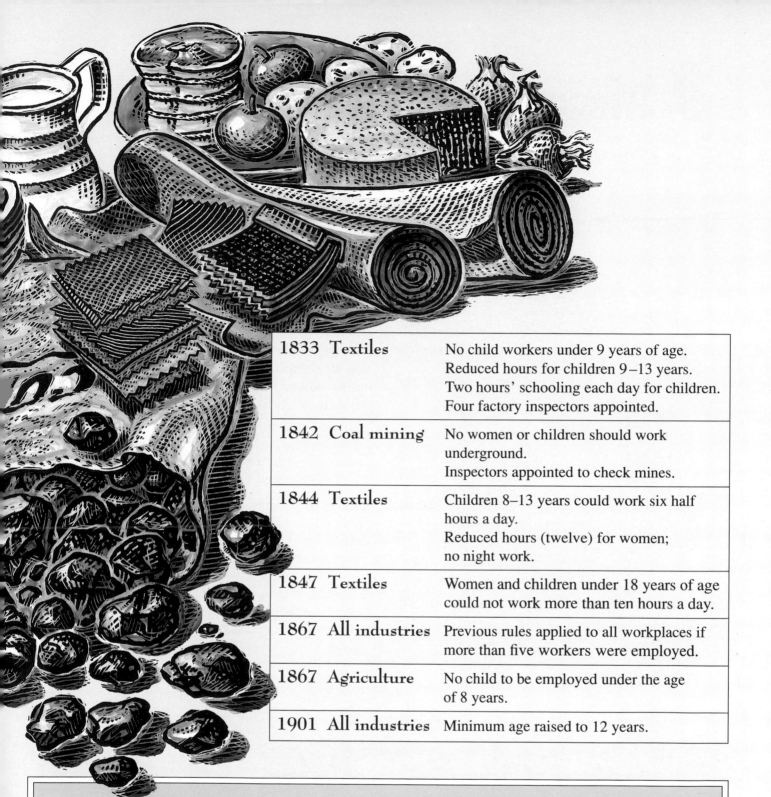

1833 Textiles	No child workers under 9 years of age. Reduced hours for children 9–13 years. Two hours' schooling each day for children. Four factory inspectors appointed.
1842 Coal mining	No women or children should work underground. Inspectors appointed to check mines.
1844 Textiles	Children 8–13 years could work six half hours a day. Reduced hours (twelve) for women; no night work.
1847 Textiles	Women and children under 18 years of age could not work more than ten hours a day.
1867 All industries	Previous rules applied to all workplaces if more than five workers were employed.
1867 Agriculture	No child to be employed under the age of 8 years.
1901 All industries	Minimum age raised to 12 years.

1 Draw two columns, one headed *Mill* and the other headed *Mine*.

a Using Sources A to D, list the many problems or complaints in the mills.

b Use Sources E to H to do the same for mines.

2 Some sources show clearly that people at the time considered the treatment of working children to be wrong. Which of the sources in this unit show this attitude most clearly? How do they do this?

3 Using information from this unit, write a speech for a Member of Parliament in 1830 either for or against children being allowed to work in mills and factories.

4 Explain in your own words how children were gradually banned by law from working.

9 Winners and losers

The lives of ordinary people were greatly changed by the coming of the factory age. More and more people left the land and got new jobs in the growing towns and cities.

Did life get better or worse for ordinary people during these years?

An argument among historians

In recent years British historians have had a long-running disagreement about the standard of living of ordinary working families in the years after 1750. Some feel that life got better for people, others say that the quality of life got worse.

Wages and prices

Most historians agree that *real wages* increased between 1750 and 1900. This meant that, on average, people could buy more with their money. Many working people were able to improve their diet and buy a few 'luxury' goods. After 1750 most people insisted on buying quality wheat bread instead of a lower-grade mix of wheat, barley and rye. The purchase of tea, sugar, soap and other goods increased.

A general rise in wages hides lots of differences from job to job. Factory workers were much better paid than farm workers. Between 1815 and 1850 unskilled factory workers were paid about 18 shillings (90p) a week, compared to about 9 shillings (45p) for farm workers. A skilled male worker in a cotton mill would earn up to 25 shillings (£1.25p). Skilled workers in specialised trades, such as printing, could earn 40 shillings (£2.00) a week. In other words, some workers were paid four times more than others.

The well-being of working people varied from time to time. The years 1793–1815 were difficult ones because Britain was at war with France and during the war the price of food increased dramatically.

In 1811, when prices were at their highest, some textile workers in Nottinghamshire and Yorkshire were threatened with unemployment because of new machines. There was an outbreak of machine-breaking by workers who called themselves Luddites (after an imaginary leader, Ned Ludd). The Luddite movement soon faded away but it showed how desperate some workers became when prices were high.

Source A

Awaiting Admission to the Casual Ward *by Sir Luke Fildes. This shows poor people waiting to go into the workhouse.*

● *How can you tell that the artist sympathised with the poor?*

Prisons for the poor

Rising wages were of little use to those out of work. In 1834, the government introduced a new system to deal with people who could not support themselves because of unemployment, old age or sickness. Workhouses were built across the country. Inside the workhouses families were split up, people were given a workhouse uniform and were treated very strictly. Workhouse food was basic and monotonous, smoking and drinking were not allowed, and people were given particularly boring jobs such as breaking stones. Not surprisingly, the workhouses were unpopular among working people. Although most people did not have to go to workhouses, it always threatened if a worker became sick or unemployed. Workhouses were like prisons and it seemed as if being poor had become a crime.

The hand-loom weavers

Cloth is woven on a loom. After 1800 more and more weaving was done in factories on large machines called power-looms. The weavers who used the old method of weaving on a hand-loom at home were in trouble. Wages fell very quickly from an average of £1 a week in 1800 to little more than five shillings (25p) a week by the 1830s.

Source B

The poverty of the hand-loom weavers was so bad that the government produced a report on their plight. This interview took place when Members of Parliament were gathering information:

'Question: You are a weaver?
Answer: Yes.
Question: How does the fall in wages affect you?
Answer: It robs me of all the comforts of life. I can get nothing but the worst of food and less of it than I used to.
Question: What do you do for furniture?
Answer: I have never bought any in my life.'

Select Committee on Hand-loom Weavers, 1834

The birth of trade unions

Between 1750 and 1900 many workers tried to make their lives better by forming trade unions. By joining together they hoped to get better wages and conditions from their employers. At first these early unions were not very successful. The government did not like unions and they were made illegal in 1799. It was not until 1825 that the law was changed and people were allowed to join unions under a number of strict controls. During the next few years many new unions were formed but most of them soon failed. In 1834 a huge union was set up called the Grand National Consolidated Trades Union (GNCTU). This union only lasted a few months before it fell apart. Six farm workers from Tolpuddle in Dorset who tried to join the GNCTU were transported to Australia for breaking an old law about making secret oaths or promises. These men became known as the Tolpuddle Martyrs.

It was not until the 1850s and 1860s that trade unions finally began to establish themselves. The new unions of these years organised skilled craft workers and represented the better-paid employees. In 1868 these new unions joined together to form the Trades Union Congress, which has been the national voice of the trade union movement ever since. It was only at the end of the nineteenth century that badly paid, unskilled workers set up successful unions. In 1888 badly paid women who made matches in dangerous conditions staged a successful strike. A year later the London dockers went on strike for a basic wage of 6d (2.5p) an hour. The dockers won their pay rise and this encouraged more unskilled workers to join unions. By 1900 trade unions had about 2 million members.

Source C
Trade union banner.

1 Some historians think that life got better for working people after 1750, while others believe that life got worse. Produce and fill in a table under the following headings using information from this unit:
Evidence that life was getting better
Evidence that life was getting worse

2 Why do you think it is that historians disagree about whether life was getting better or worse?

3 You are a historian. You have been commissioned by a magazine to write an article on the lives of working people between 1750 and 1900. Use this unit and other units in this book to provide your evidence. Explain whether you think life got better or worse during these years.

10 Squalor and splendour

Some towns and cities grew greatly in size. For the poor, life in these towns was often grim. The rich erected magnificent new buildings.

What was life like in the industrial towns and cities?

Conditions in the towns

In the growing industrial towns and cities many of the workers who were producing the wealth of the nation lived in conditions of squalor and poverty lacking what we would consider to be the basic necessities of life.

Source A

This writer describes his horror as he saw some of the worst conditions in London:

'We were led to a narrow, closed court, where the sun never shone. We then passed along the reeking banks of the sewer. In the bright light the water appeared the colour of strong green tea. Indeed, it was more like watery mud than muddy water, and yet we were told this was the only water the wretched people had to drink. As we gazed in horror at the pool, we saw drains and sewers emptying their filthy contents into it. We heard children bathing in it.

In this wretched place we were taken to a house where an infant lay dead of the cholera. We asked if they really did drink the water. The answer was, "We have to drink from the ditch unless we can beg or steal a bucketful of the river Thames."'

Henry Mayhew, *Life and Labour of the London People*, 1861

Source B

The Cellar *by John Leech, 1850.*

● *This picture shows conditions in a cellar home. Who do you think the man in the top hat might be? Notice the animals in the room. What other signs can you see of poverty and unhealthy conditions?*

Source C

This is a report by a doctor on the city of Newcastle upon Tyne:

'In some of the courts I have noticed heaps of filth which, when it rains, get into the cellar dwellings. Stagnant ditches may be seen near most of the houses, and house drains, where they exist, have not been built properly and often become choked. In many houses a whole family shares one room.'

Dr D. B. Reid, Report on the Sanitary Conditions of Newcastle, 1845

● Why do you think that so many houses were built with no proper drainage and water supply?

Source D

An engraving of terraced houses in London by Gustave Doré, 1872.

Disease

Killer diseases, such as consumption, typhus and cholera, spread rapidly in conditions like these. Doctors knew the symptoms of these diseases and recognised that poor diet and overcrowding were closely connected with them. However, until the second half of the nineteenth century they knew nothing of germs and how they were transmitted to people. In particular, they did not know that cholera was spread by water supplies which had come into contact with human excrement.

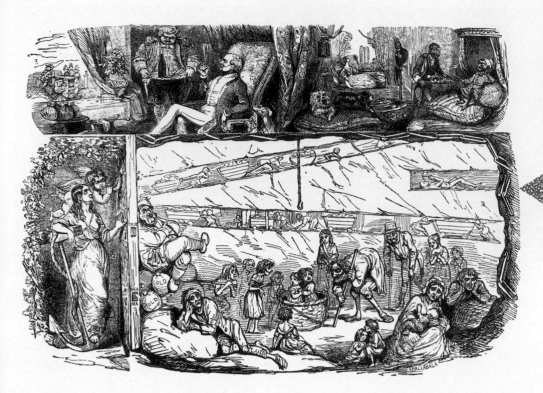

Urban splendour

While many people in the cities lived in squalor, huge sums of money were spent on magnificent buildings. What can we learn from the great buildings of the time?

Source E

Capital and Labour – *a* Punch *cartoon.*

● *What point is the artist making about the relationship between the rich and the poor?*

Source F

Leeds Town Hall, built in 1859.

● *What do you think town halls were used for? Try to think of a reason why certain types of people would want their town hall to look very grand.*

Source G

The Halifax Town Hall, West Yorkshire

● *What words would you use to describe this building? What does the building tell us about the importance of the activities which took place inside it?*

1 Basing your answer on Sources A–D, make a list of all the problems of living in towns in the nineteenth century.

2 What sort of buildings in cities did rich businessmen spend their money on?

3 Why do you think buildings like those shown in Sources F and G survive today while most of the houses of the poor have been destroyed?

4 Imagine that you and your family have just moved from the country to a big industrial city to get a job in a factory. Write a letter home to your relatives describing the big city.

11 Religion

In 1750 the Anglican Church dominated many areas of life. By 1900 the position of the Anglicans had been weakened in many ways.

How did the position of the Anglican Church change?

In the 1750s the British Isles were deeply divided by religion. There were three main religious groups: Anglicans, Dissenters and Catholics. They did not get on well together. These divisions dated back to the sixteenth and seventeenth centuries. In Ireland, Wales and England there was an official Anglican Church with many special privileges. The other groups bitterly resented the power of the Anglicans.

Britain gradually became a more tolerant country in the years after 1750. These are some of the milestones on the road to greater tolerance.

The special position of the Anglican Church in 1750.

Only Anglicans could be MPs and government ministers.

Catholics were not allowed to vote in elections.

Catholics and Dissenters were not allowed to be army officers.

Only Anglicans could go to university.

Catholics and Dissenters were not allowed to serve on town councils.

The Anglican Churches were in charge of registering every birth, marriage and death.

The fall of Anglican privilege.

1793 Catholics are allowed to vote.

1828 Dissenters are allowed full political rights.

1829 Catholics are allowed to become Members of Parliament and government ministers.

1836 Births, marriages and deaths are to be registered by the government, not the Anglican Church.

1858 Jews are allowed to become Members of Parliament.

1871 Dissenters and Catholics are allowed to go to university.

The decline of belief

In 1851 a special census of religions took place on one Sunday in that year to see how many people went to church. Over half of the population did not got to church at all; in inner-city areas as many as 90% of the population did not attend church.

Source A

The religious census of 1851. Figures for selected areas.

	% population at Anglican service	% population at Dissenters' service	% population at Catholic service	% population not at church
London	14.0	9.1	1.6	75.3
South West	25.3	22.9	0.3	51.5
Yorkshire	13.0	22.5	1.1	63.4
Wales	10.6	44.0	0.5	44.9

Source B ▼

A cartoon of Charles Darwin with an ape.

● *What point is the cartoonist making?*

The challenge of science

New scientific thinking created more problems for the Churches. In 1859 the scientist, Charles Darwin, published his book on evolution, *The Origin of Species,* which challenged the story of the creation of the world found in the Bible. Many educated people were forced to rethink their basic beliefs.

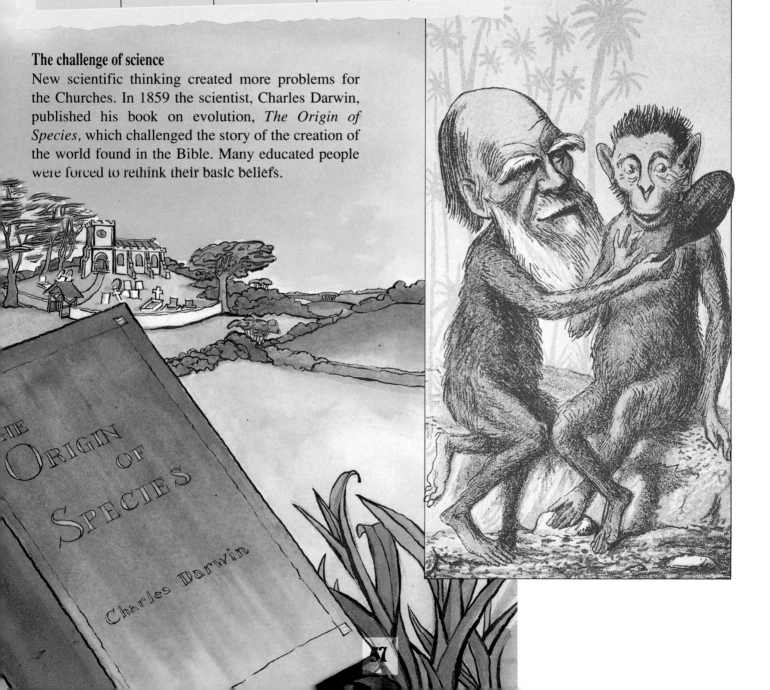

Methodism

A new Dissenters' Church arose in eighteenth-century Britain that also challenged the position of the Anglican Church. This new religious movement became known as Methodism. It was founded by John Wesley and he and his followers took the Christian message to the new areas of the growing industrial towns and mining areas. The Anglican Church had largely ignored the people of these new settlements. Methodism also appealed to many farm workers who saw the Anglican Church as a rich man's club. The impact of Methodism varied from place to place and was particularly strong in Wales, Cornwall and the northern factory towns.

The Methodist movement grew very rapidly and there were a quarter of a million Methodists in Great Britain by 1815. Many working people, in both town and countryside, preferred Methodism to the ways of the Anglican Church.

Methodism gained strong support in the rapidly changing industrial communities for the following reasons:

1 John Wesley reached large numbers of people by travelling around the country and preaching, not in churches, but in the open air.

2 Wesley's message was very simple and straightforward. He wanted people to take their religion much more seriously and to be whole-hearted in leading a Christian life.

3 Wesley's preaching was very powerful and affected many people very deeply. It was also exciting and dramatic and quite unlike anything people would have heard in church.

4 Methodists were very well organised with local groups set up in each area.

5 Methodism allowed working people to become group leaders and preachers.

Source C

A labourer, born in 1870, explained why his family chose to go to a Methodist chapel rather than the Church of England:

'It seemed as if we had more of a right to be there than we had in church, what was run by the big farmers and the rich folk. The parsons at the church, with their educated voices and their long words, were a queer lot, and thought theirselves a lot better than the folk they were supposed to serve. Whenever we met the parson or his wife, we had to stop and touch our caps and bow our heads, and the girls would have to curtsy.'

Source D

Wesley preaching from his father's tomb.

The Anglicans fight back

Within the Anglican Church a new spirit appeared towards the end of the eighteenth century. This was known as the Evangelical movement. Many better-off Anglicans became very serious about religion and their obligations to poorer people. These Evangelicals played an important part in the campaign to end slavery and child labour in factories. They wanted to follow the Methodists and take Christianity to the people of the new industrial towns. The Anglican Church in England built 1,750 new churches between 1840 and 1876.

---

1 a What privileges did Anglicans have in 1750?

b Why do you think Catholics and Dissenters disliked these privileges?

2 What happened to the special position of Anglicans between 1750 and 1900?

3 Who were the Methodists and why did their Church spread so quickly?

4 Look at Source A. Why did the religious census of 1851 shock many Christians?

12 On the move

In the nineteenth century millions of Europeans left home and started life in another country. Nearly 12 million people left Britain, either for the United States of America or for parts of the British Empire. Also, many chose to come to Britain, such as Jews from Eastern Europe and over 1.5 million Irish people. Most of the emigrants, whether leaving or arriving in Britain, chose to emigrate because of economic hardship at home.

What was it like to leave one's homeland and settle in a strange country?

Leaving Britain

Leaving familiar surroundings and saying goodbye to friends and family is never an easy thing to do, even if you are confidently looking forward to a better life thousands of miles away. If we look closely at some sources for the nineteenth century we can begin to imagine what it must have been like to do this then.

Source A

A Victorian clergyman described what he saw whilst visiting the port of Liverpool:

'As we came down the river several large emigrant ships lay in the river getting up steam. Small steam boats kept bringing fresh loads of passengers alongside the big ships. One could not help thinking of the hundreds of sorrowful hearts on board and ashore and the farewells and partings for. ever, on this side of the grave.'

Kilvert's Diary, 1872

● Why would many people leaving their homeland at this time not have expected to see their relatives again? Why would communications have been very difficult?

Source B

The Emigrant Ship *by Charles Staniland.*

● *Many Victorian artists used the idea of leaving home in their paintings. Why do you think that this was a popular choice of subject?*

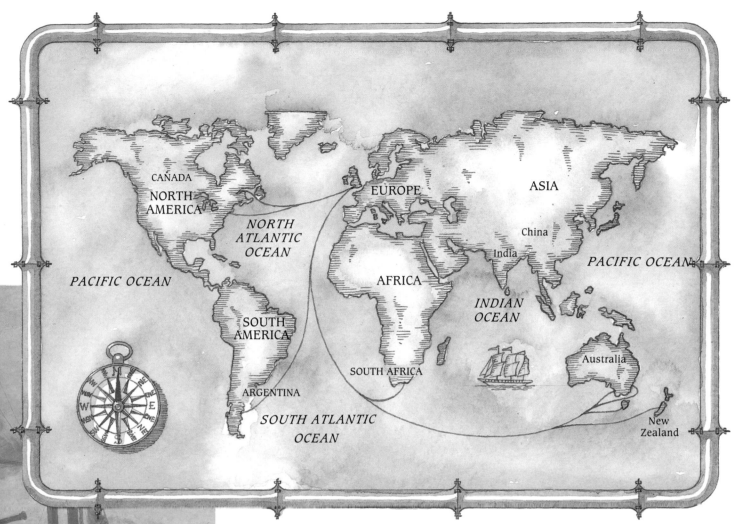

Where did they go?

This map shows you the places where most British emigrants were heading.

● Which of these places belonged to the British Empire in the nineteenth century?

Why did they go?

Numbers of people leaving Britain increased rapidly during the 1830s and 1840s. These were years when many working people experienced serious difficulties caused by low wages or unemployment and high bread prices. In the 1820s, 193,000 people left Britain, but in the 1830s this figure rose to 671,000.

Source C

A modern historian shows how the numbers of emigrants seem to be affected by the amount of hardship at home. In the years 1830 to 1832 it was particularly hard for labourers and their families to earn a living:

'The emigration figures for 1830 show a sudden increase to 60,000 a year from the previous maximum of 30,000 a year. In 1832 it was over 100,000. The annual average for the three years 1847–9 was well over 250,000. However, the *push* was always more important than the *pull*: in the years 1844–5, when corn was cheap, emigration slackened.'

David Thoms, *England in the Nineteenth Century*, 1950

● What do you think the writer of Source C means by *push* and *pull*?

Emigrating to the colonies

Some people left hoping to buy farms because land was cheap in the United States of America, Canada and Australia. Others were lured by the promise of higher wages. The British government was very keen to encourage large numbers of the poorest and unskilled labourers to leave the country. They were also particularly anxious that people should choose to go to British colonies. In 1835, a grant of £20 was made to any young married labourer wanting to go to Australia. However, as these figures show, the United States of America became the most popular destination in the late nineteenth century.

	USA	Canada	Australia	Other
1871–80	44,200	90,000	184,000	37,000
1881–90	1,088,000	257,000	317,000	162,000

Source D

Here and There, *a* Punch *cartoon, 1840.*

● *This cartoon made fun of the government's messages about emigration by suggesting that the government might have been exaggerating. How does it do this?*

The Irish Famine

In February 1847, a steamship sailed into a village in the south-west of Ireland. Her captain, Commander Caffyn, wrote a report on what he saw:

'Corpses lay on the ground, half eaten by dogs. Children had strangely swollen stomachs and jaws so deformed they could not speak. Their skin was covered in black blotches caused by scurvy. People wandered about aimlessly, often naked and driven mad with hunger.'

Source E

A scene from the Irish Famine.

The Great Irish Famine was caused by the failure of the potato crop in the mid 1840s. By 1851 over a million Irish people had emigrated to America and one and a half million had fled to Britain and other parts of the world where they struggled to find work. The British census of 1881 shows the Irish clustered in three main areas: London, northern manufacturing and mining towns and the Glasgow area.

Settling in Britain

British people have always been a mix of different races and cultures. Nevertheless, when groups arrive in large numbers they are often treated with hatred and suspicion. In the nineteenth century, as well as the rapid increase in the numbers of Irish immigrants, there was also a sharp increase in Jewish immigration. Jews began to be persecuted in Russia and Eastern Europe in the 1880s and many fled to Britain or the United States of America. These sources reveal some of the experiences of immigrants in Britain.

Source F

Prejudice against Jews was often expressed in the press:

'People of any other nation, after being in England a short time, blend in with the native race and by and by lose nearly all their foreign trace. But the Jews never do.'

East London Advertiser, 1899

Source G

A modern history book takes a different view:

'Jews readily adapted to urban and industrial life. This helped to become part of British society, though at the price of weakening their traditional customs and religion.'

Colin Ford and Brian Harrison, *Britain in the 1880s, 1983*

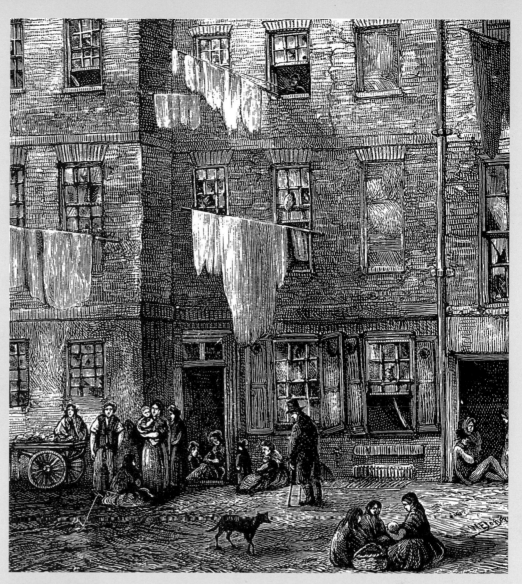

Source H

Nineteenth-century street scene in an Irish area of London.

The desire of the Irish immigrants to stay together meant that parts of some cities were soon almost entirely Irish. Their willingness to take low-paid jobs meant that those areas had the lowest rents and worst housing. Why do you think that their willingness to work for low pay also brought hostility from other working people?

1 a Why did so many British people emigrate in this period?
b Where did the emigrants go?

2 What can we learn from a painting like Source B?

3 Think of as many reasons as you can why the British government wanted:
a poor people to emigrate;
b people to emigrate to British colonies;
c married people to emigrate to British colonies.
Now try to use information from other chapters to support your answer.

4 Why do you think immigrants like the Irish and the Jews were so badly treated?

13 The role of women

Changes in industry were carried out by women as well as men.
The majority of workers in the new cotton factories were women.
Women began a long fight for equality in these years.

What was life like for women?

In the years 1750–1900 many people felt that women should not go out to work but should stay at home to look after their families.

Source A

An extract from a poem written by a well-known poet in 1847:

'Man for the field and woman for the hearth;
Man for the sword, and for the needle she;
Man with the head and woman with the heart;
Man to command and woman to obey;
All else confusion.'

Alfred Lord Tennyson, *The Princess*

● What do you think is meant by 'woman for the hearth' and 'woman with the heart'?

Source B

In 1848 a novel about the poor in Manchester was published. The author was a woman from the middle classes. Here is a conversation taken from the story:

'"Father does not like girls to work in factories," said Mary. "And with good reason," replied Mrs Wilson. "They oughtn't to do that after they're married, that I'm very clear about. I could count nine men I know, as have been driven to the public house by having wives that worked in factories; good folk too, that thought there was no harm in putting their little ones out to nurse, and letting their house go all dirty, and their fires all out; and that was a place that was tempting for a husband to stay in was it? He soon finds gin-shops, where all is clean and bright, and where the fire blazes cheerfully, and gives a man a welcome."'

Elizabeth Gaskell, *Mary Barton*, 1848

● Who does Mrs Wilson blame for encouraging men to spend their time in pubs?

Despite these views, women played a vital part in the economy. Before they got married, virtually all working-class women went out to work.

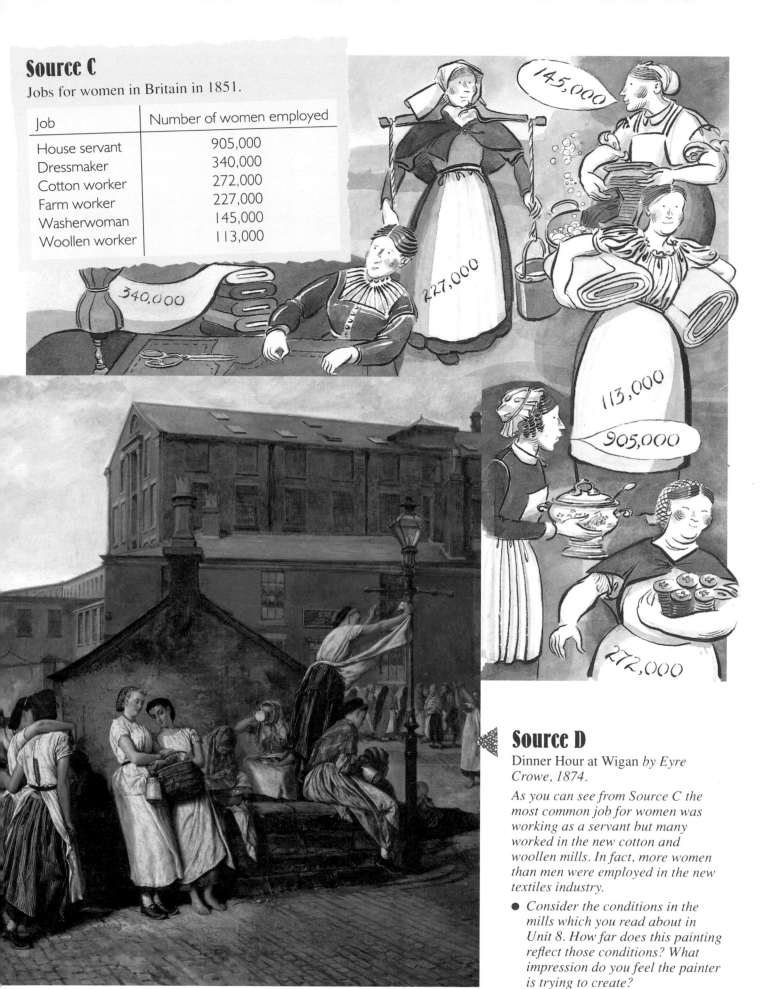

Source C

Jobs for women in Britain in 1851.

Job	Number of women employed
House servant	905,000
Dressmaker	340,000
Cotton worker	272,000
Farm worker	227,000
Washerwoman	145,000
Woollen worker	113,000

Source D

Dinner Hour at Wigan *by Eyre Crowe, 1874.*

As you can see from Source C the most common job for women was working as a servant but many worked in the new cotton and woollen mills. In fact, more women than men were employed in the new textiles industry.

- *Consider the conditions in the mills which you read about in Unit 8. How far does this painting reflect those conditions? What impression do you feel the painter is trying to create?*

The Victorian family

Many Victorian writers and painters showed home and family as the source of all happiness and goodness. Many pictures were painted of Queen Victoria, her husband and children as an example of the ideal family.

The task of the 'angel in the house', as one Victorian described the role of woman, was to hold family life together by caring and setting a good example. This view of a woman's role created a problem for middle-class women who were unmarried and therefore needed to earn a living. Very few jobs were considered proper or 'respectable' for such women. Those that were considered respectable usually had some connection with children or caring such as teaching or, towards the end of the nineteenth century, nursing.

Second-class citizens

Women were undoubtedly second-class citizens. They were banned from most well-paid jobs such as being a doctor, lawyer or civil servant. Universities would not allow them in as students. Divorce was practically impossible and many women were trapped in unhappy marriages. Married women had no property of their own as everything they had was considered to belong to their husbands.

Some improvement in the position of women took place between 1850 and 1900. Divorce became more widely available after 1857. In the 1850s, two famous schools for middle-class girls were opened: the North London Collegiate School and Cheltenham Ladies' College. A campaign to get women into university led by Emily Davies was finally successful in 1869 when Girton College, Cambridge, opened. After 1870 women were allowed by law to keep their own property after marriage. Despite these changes, men retained their dominant role in society and by 1900 women were still not allowed to vote.

Source E
Portrait of Queen Victoria and her children.

Images of women

What can we learn about the position of women from the following pictures?

Source F

Carting Turf from the Moss *by Thomas Wade*.

- *Many women worked as farm labourers. Life for many poor women in the countryside was extremely hard, just as it was in towns. What clues does this picture give about the kinds of difficulty that such women might have faced?*

Source G

Washing Day *by Pierre Édouard Frere.*

● *How does the painting help us to understand why it must have been very difficult to combine running a home with outside work? This is a fairly cheerful painting (compared with Source F, for example).*

What impression does the artist give of this washing day? Is there anything about the painting which strikes you as unrealistic?

Source H

Conversation Piece *by Joseph Solomon, 1884.*

● *Which social class do you think these people are from?*
How can you tell? What are the two women doing?
What was the role of the two women in the
background? In what ways do you think their
experience might have been different from that of the
other women in the picture?

1 'In Victorian times people believed that
women should not go out to work.' Using
Sources A, B and C explain whether you
agree with this statement.

2 How did the position of women change
between 1850 and 1900?

3 a What can we learn from Sources F–H
about women in the nineteenth century?
b Are pictures like these more useful than
written sources?

14 Growing up

The experience of boys and girls in this period depended greatly on how rich or poor their parents were or if they had any parents at all. For children of all classes there were some important changes in the period 1750–1900.

What was it like to be a child during this period?

A classical education?

In 1750 most children did not go to school. Male children of the very rich went to the famous public schools, like Eton, Harrow and Winchester. These were violent places in the eighteenth century and the boys were taught virtually nothing except some Greek and Latin. Some middle-class boys went to boarding schools.

Source A

In the novel *Nicholas Nickleby*, Charles Dickens describes the brutal conditions to be found in some boarding schools. In this extract, Squeers, the teacher, beats a boy called Bolder because the boy has warts on his hands:

'"I can't help it, indeed, sir," rejoined the boy, crying. "They will come."
"Bolder," said Squeers, tucking up his wristbands, and moistening the palm of his right hand to get a good grip of the cane, "you are an incorrigible scoundrel, and as the last thrashing did you no good, we must see what another will do towards beating it out of you."'

Charles Dickens, *Nicholas Nickleby*, 1839

Source B

The Dame's School, 1899, *by Frederick Daniel Hardy*.

● *Dame schools were run in their own homes by women who did not need to be qualified and who often taught very little to the children. Dame schools were places where poor children could be left while their parents were working.*

Rising standards

Standards in boarding and day schools for better-off children improved during the nineteenth century. Boys were given a more balanced education with science, modern languages and history being added to Greek and Latin. Organised games like rugby and cricket played an increasingly important part.

Schools for the poor

Before the 1830s the government had almost no involvement in providing education. Politicians thought that schools should be run by the churches or charities, not by the government. After 1833, the government provided some money to help schools pay their bills. The amount of government money spent on education grew steadily over the next thirty years. New elementary schools were set up for ordinary children. These schools taught simple mathematics, English, reading and writing and almost nothing else. Despite these new schools it was still possible for children not to have a local school until, in 1870, the government set up school boards to provide education in all areas. It was not until 1880 that a law was passed forcing all children to go to school until they were ten years old.

Source C

Rugby School, a boys' public school.

Source D

A late nineteenth-century schoolroom for working-class girls.

Source E

This is an extract from the unpublished autobiography of Jack Lanigan. The writer was born in Salford, Lancashire, in 1890. His father, a skilled worker, died while he and his brother were very young:

'"'Ave yer any bread left, master?" That was the theme song of hundreds of youngsters of whom my brother Matt and I could be counted. We stood outside the gates of Mather and Platt Ltd, waiting for the gates to open at 6 p.m. When they did, the workers would file out into the street carrying their wicker lunch baskets and when they heard our voices they would hand anything they had left out to us. When I had got sufficient for my mother and brother, I made tracks for home and these left-overs would be shared with a cup of tea; if no tea then a cup of water.

The days of 1890 to 1900 were tough. One cannot go to bed hungry and get up in the morning with that same feeling without leaving a scar on the memory.

The back bedroom, where Matt and I slept, was immediately over a large dung heap from a six-seater lavatory. The smell in our bedroom was vile. I cannot remember having any bedding on our bed. The coverings to cover our little bodies were old coats and sacks. If ever I was invited to the house of a playmate, their beds were similar.'

Source F

An extract from the unpublished autobiography of Alice Foley. She too was born in Lancashire, in 1891. She was the sixth child in her family. Her father drank heavily and was often out of work:

'We were brought up mainly out of my mother's wash-tub earnings. Frequently, I accompanied her to various better-off houses, and sitting on the floor amongst a pile of dirty clothes, played games and chattered aloud whilst she silently scrubbed shirts or mangled heavy sheets.'

Source G

Many Happy Returns *by W. P. Frith, 1856.*

- *Children such as those in the picture would have had a very different experience from those described in Sources E and F and those in the photograph of Dr Barnardo's children. What sort of differences can you think of?*

Source H ▲

Dr Barnardo's children being taught a trade.

- *Thomas John Barnardo trained as a medical missionary. He set up a mission for destitute children and helped thousands of homeless children in Victorian cities.*

---

1 What was wrong with the school system in 1750?

2 How did schools change between 1750 and 1900?

3 'Rich and poor children led very different lives.' Using information from this unit explain whether you agree with this statement.

15 The real world of work?

Much of our understanding of the past comes from the work of artists, musicians, poets and novelists.

Do the artists of the nineteenth century create a clear picture of what life was like for working people during this period?

Rural bliss or hard times?

Myles Birket Foster was one of the most popular of late Victorian painters. *The Lacemaker* is typical of his work. It shows a traditional countryside or cottage industry. How does the artist create a pleasant and peaceful image? What can this tell us about the views and attitudes of people at this time? By the time Foster was painting, cottage industries were already dying out. Flora Thompson, in her description of village life in the 1880s, describes lacemaking as a skill which was only known by old women. She said that one old lady complained, 'This nasty machine-made stuff has killed all the lacemaking.' Glovemaking was a similar cottage industry.

Source A

The Lacemaker *by Myles Birket Foster.*

● *Many other artists tried to copy this style because such paintings were so popular with critics and those people who bought paintings. Why do you think they were popular?*

Source B ▶

A photograph of Mrs Brackenborough, glovemaker, taken in Woodstock, Oxfordshire, in 1900.

● *In some ways the subject of this photograph is remarkably similar to that of Source A. In what ways, however, does the photograph give a completely different impression of life? Are the impressions different simply because the first is a painting and the second is a photograph?*

Source C

Hard Times *by Sir Hubert von Herkomer, 1885.*

In the 1870s and 1880s some painters were concerned at the number of unemployed rural workers, who often had to walk long distances seeking work. Sir Hubert von Herkomer painted Hard Times *in 1885, having seen such a family resting on their journey, near his home in Bushey, Hertfordshire.*

● *Contrast the impression made by this painting with the one made by Source A. You have seen that Source A was painted in a popular style. How might Victorian society have reacted to the image portrayed in* Hard Times?

Source D

Work *by Ford Maddox Brown, painted in 1863.*

- *The central figures of the painting are road workers. Why do you think the artist has made the labourers look heroic and important? Do you think this scene presents a realistic picture of what hard manual work was really like?*

Source E

Children carrying heavy wet clay in a brickyard.

● *Do you think this picture of work is more realistic than the scene in Source D? Why do you think the artist wanted to show children working in these conditions?*

1 What different kinds of work are depicted in Sources A–E?

2 Do you think that some of the images presented are more realistic than others?

3 How are these pictures useful to the historian?

POWER & AUTHORITY

In the eighteenth century only three adults in a hundred could vote. Only the rich became Members of Parliament and most of these were landowners from southern England. The king still had a lot of influence over how the government acted.

King Louis XVI of France was beheaded in 1793 during the French Revolution. The events in France between 1789 and 1815 made British governments very nervous about the possibility of a revolution in England so any protests or opposition involving working people were dealt with very harshly.

In 1819 about 60,000 people gathered in Manchester to hear Henry Hunt speak in favour of 'votes for all'. The peaceful meeting ended violently when troops rode into the crowd, killing 11 people. The event became known as the Peterloo Massacre.

The industrial revolution led to a growth in Britain's middle class. As these people became more wealthy and influential, the political system came under pressure to include them.

Protests about the unfairness of the political system from the emerging middle class helped to win the first reform of parliament in 1832. The way British Members of Parliament were elected was changed as a new law was passed on elections and constituencies.

The 1832 Reform Act disappointed many working people because they still had no political power. A group of London working men drew up a charter of six political reforms in 1836 – this was the beginning of the Chartist movement.

After 1832 the Whig and Tory parties began to behave more like modern political parties. The role of government began to change as parliament began to interfere more in the economic and social affairs of the country.

In 1867 and 1884 more men were given the right to vote. Voting now took place in secret as strict rules were passed to stop cheating at elections. Women still did not have the right to vote. Nearly all MPs belonged to a political party – either Conservative or Liberal. In 1893 the Independent Labour Party was formed to represent working people in parliament.

16 Power and the people

You have seen how great the changes were in the way British people lived and worked in the period after 1750. However, the way in which Britain was governed had not changed since the seventeenth century.

Why were many people unhappy with this political system?

The power of the aristocracy

In the seventeenth century Britain had been torn apart by a violent disagreement about who should rule the country. The winners in this bitter struggle were the landed aristocrats, who owned much of the countryside. Between 1688 and 1832 these rich land-lords controlled parliament. There was no real democracy: all women and most men were barred from voting.

Aristocrats dominated both the House of Lords and the House of Commons. Elections to the House of Commons were very different from today. There were a very few constituencies, such as Preston and Coventry, where most men were allowed to vote but these were very much the exception. In many more constituencies only a small number of wealthy men could vote: in 1830 there were 77 seats which each had less than a hundred votes. In the Cornish con-stituency of Helston, for example, only 19 men had the vote. In 1793 it was calculated that about 11,000 men were entitled to elect over half of all Members of Parliament.

These electors were often prepared, in return for favours, to elect a man chosen by the greatest landowner of the area. In 1827 it was calculated that about half of all Members of Parliament had been chosen or nominated by a powerful landowner. When in parliament these MPs did as they were told by the landowners who had chosen them. The system was so undemocratic that much of the time nobody bothered to stand against the selected candidate and he would be elected without a contest.

A modern artist's impression of the abuse of the electoral system.

Source A

An Election Entertainment *by William Hogarth.*

Election day

Elections were very different from our own modern elections and life for the voter was difficult. Hogarth's picture shows fighting, with voters being pressed into voting for one candidate or another. Bribery was common. Evidence suggests that prices for a person's vote varied from £2 to £30. There was no secrecy for the voter so it was easy to bully or bribe him.

The industrial changes of the eighteenth century made the voting system even more unfair. The population increased many times between 1700 and 1830, but the number of voters remained unchanged. The great new industrial cities of Birmingham, Leeds, Manchester and Sheffield did not have Members of Parliament. At the same time, a tiny village in Suffolk called Dunwich, which had been an important town in the Middle Ages, elected 2 MPs although it consisted of only 44 houses.

Critics of the system

We do need to remember that this unfairness did not seem quite so ridiculous at the time as it does to us. Most Members of Parliament saw themselves as representing land or property rather than people. It therefore seemed sensible that only owners of large amounts of land could vote. However, by the early nineteenth century the ownership of property and the movement of population had changed so much that an increasing number of people began to comment on the unfairness of the system. Most voters were very wealthy, but the system was so complicated that this varied from town to town. Important changes were necessary if the new kinds of wealth and property created by the industrial revolution were to be represented in parliament.

Source C

The Storming of the Bastille, 1789.

● *Revolutions in other countries, like France, made the British government anxious that democratic reforms might lead to similar uprisings in Britain.*

Source B

This extract shows how the movement of population had made the system of representation quite ridiculous:

'The county of Yorkshire, which contains nearly a million people, sends two county MPs and so does Rutland, which has less than one per cent of that number. The town of Old Sarum, which contains no more than three houses, sends two MPs and the town of Manchester, which has more than sixty thousand people, is not allowed to send any.'

Tom Paine, *The Rights of Man*, 1791

Moves to reform parliament were delayed by a series of wars and rebellions. Britain was at war with her American colonies from 1775 to 1783 and with revolutionary France from 1793 to 1815. In 1798 a group of Irish people staged an armed rebellion against British rule. These rebels and revolutionaries argued for more democratic government. The British government became very defensive and suspicious of any suggestions of change in the way parliament was elected.

---

1 Which of the following groups was the most powerful in the eighteenth century?
◆ rich businessmen
◆ rich landowners
◆ rich women

2 Why were people in big northern cities like Leeds and Manchester unhappy in 1800 with the way MPs were elected?

3 Would you say that Britain was a democratic country in this period? Give reasons for your answer.

---

17 The Peterloo Massacre

In 1815 the war with France ended, but hard times followed for many people. Unemployment was high and bread was very expensive. Many protests against the political system took place. Most of these were peaceful, but in the summer of 1819 there was bloodshed in Manchester.

Who was to blame for the massacre?

Killed at Peterloo

At 1.30 a.m. on 7 September 1819, a young cotton spinner from Oldham died in agony. Three weeks beforehand he had been badly injured. His body was a mass of bruises and cuts. In spite of careful nursing by his family he became paralysed and blind, and eventually died. This man, John Lees, had been a soldier in the wars against the French. However, he was killed by his own countrymen in what became known as the 'Peterloo Massacre'.

On 16 August 1819, 60,000 men, women and children gathered at St Peter's Fields in Manchester. The day began in a peaceful atmosphere. Bands played as groups marched carrying banners with slogans such as *Votes for All*. They had come to hear Henry 'Orator' Hunt, a famous speaker, criticise the government. Just as he was speaking, the magistrates ordered volunteer soldiers – the yeomanry – to arrest him. This caused uproar. Troops rode into the crowd and panic broke out. In just ten minutes eleven people were killed and hundreds injured. Four years earlier Britain had been proud of her part in the victory against France at the battle of Waterloo. Now critics of the government created the name 'Peterloo' to show their disgust at what had taken place.

Source A

Britons Strike Home *by George Cruikshank which shows a contemporary cartoonist's view of the Peterloo Massacre.*

Source B

This is an extract from the statement of a witness at John Lees' inquest:

'When I got to the end of Watson Street, I saw ten or twelve of the cavalry cutting at the people. An officer rode up to his own men and shouted, "For shame, gentlemen, what are you doing? The people cannot get away." They stopped for a time, but as soon as the officer rode off they began again.'

Source C

A description by an officer of the cavalry, Lieutenant Joliffe:

'Although nine out of ten of the sword wounds were caused by the cavalry, it was a tribute to the patience of the troops that more wounds were not received. The largest number of injuries were from the pressure of the huge crowd in panic.'

Source D

Some of the Peterloo casualties which were recorded afterwards:

Name	Age	Trade	Comments
Elizabeth Adshead	43	–	Ribs and body injured when trampled on by the crowd.
John Ainsworth	24	Weaver	Severe sword cut on his right cheek.
William Alcock	55	Ironworker	Right arm cut by a soldier's sword.
Samuel Ackerley	61	Tailor	Sword cut on left leg.
Thomas Blumstone	74	Blacksmith	Both arms badly broken. Unlikely to be able to work again.

The verdicts

Very soon after Peterloo different views were put forward about who was to blame. Were the magistrates to blame or were the people? Were the troops guilty of an unprovoked attack upon innocent people, or did the crowd's behaviour cause them to take drastic action? Many different groups of people joined in attacking the behaviour of the soldiers, including some Members of Parliament. However, the government was unmoved. It defended the magistrates and the soldiers, and introduced new laws placing even more restrictions on political freedom. The Prince Regent congratulated the magistrates on their action.

The evidence

Source E

This is an extract from a Manchester newspaper:

'The events of yesterday will bring shame upon Hunt and his colleagues and the anger of many a sorrowing family. They ignored the warnings of the Magistrates, organised a huge crowd and stirred up the people with extreme language. The necessary action of the troops has led, we regret to say, to some deaths and many very serious accidents.'

Manchester Mercury, 17 August, 1819

● **What do you think 'extreme language' might mean?**

Source F

This is a description of the Peterloo Massacre from a modern textbook:

'The local magistrates were worried by rumours of revolt and held the yeomanry in readiness. Thousands of men, women and children came to the meeting place peacefully, though with banners flying. It was an orderly and respectable gathering. Orator Hunt offered to give himself up to the magistrates before the meeting began, but this was refused and the meeting took its course. Halfway through, the magistrates decided it was illegal and sent in the yeomanry to arrest Hunt, who allowed himself to be taken without resistance. However, the yeomanry had some difficulty in reaching the platform, and were surrounded by angry protesters. They drew their sabres and another group of soldiers was sent to their assistance. The soldiers no longer used the flats of their sabres, but began to strike out in all directions. The crowd attempted to escape, and there was a general panic. In ten minutes four hundred people were wounded and eleven killed.'

H. L. Peacock, *A History of Modern Britain, 1815–1981*

1 What evidence from the sources would you select:
a if you were writing a defence of the soldiers?
b if you were writing in defence of the injured people?

2 Why do you think people today still disagree about what exactly happened at Peterloo?

3 Write the script of a radio documentary explaining what you think happened at Peterloo.

18 The Great Reform Act

In 1832 the way British Members of Parliament were elected was changed. Parliament passed a new law on elections and constituencies which became known as the Great Reform Act.

Why did parliament bring in the Reform Act in 1832?

A change of government

In the early nineteenth century there were two political parties known as the Whigs and the Tories. Although the top politicians in both parties were mostly landlords, they had different views about reform. The Tories were completely set against any changes to parliament; the Whigs were ready to bring in certain limited changes. Before 1830 the Tories had been in power for many years and so there seemed little prospect of reform.

But the Tories had problems finding a good leader in the late 1820s: between 1827 and 1830 they had four different men as prime minister. The last of these was the Duke of Wellington and he was an ineffective political leader who allowed the Tories to argue among themselves. The Tories did not do well in the general election of 1830 and in November the Whigs, led by Earl Grey, took over.

The background to change

The electoral system had been chaotic for many years, with large numbers of rotten boroughs – constituencies with only a tiny handful of voters. The House of Commons was dominated by people chosen by the great landed aristocrats. The towns, like Manchester, that had grown enormously during the previous eighty years often had no Member of Parliament. The rich businessmen of the northern towns felt cheated by a system run by landowners.

Source A Old Sarum

This reform cartoon was published in 1832. The nests were all rotten boroughs. The men to the left of the tree are Whigs; those to the right of the tree are Tories. The king is in the background.

● *With which side does the cartoonist seem to sympathise? Give reasons.*

Immediate causes of reform

While these long-term factors explain the background to the Reform Act, they do not help us to make sense of why the reform happened in the particular year of 1832. To understand the timing of the Reform Act we must look at the short-term causes of change: the events of the three or four years before 1832.

Tree; or, the Foul Nests of the Danger. Publ by E. King Chancery lane.

The Radicals

Some people wanted dramatic changes to the political system with every adult man having the vote. They were called Radicals. Working-class support for the Radicals increased considerably after 1829 with the huge surge in unemployment that year. Out-of-work people blamed the government and demanded a fairer system of elections.

The working-class Radicals were joined by better-off middle-class people who began to demand reform. In Birmingham an organisation called the Birmingham Political Union was set up in 1830 and it soon won lots of middle-class and working-class supporters. Middle-class newspapers, like the *Manchester Guardian* and the *Leeds Mercury*, joined in the calls for change.

Law and order break down

The Whigs did not have a big enough majority in the House of Commons so a general election was called in 1831 and the Whigs won. They tried to bring in a new law on elections in October 1831 but the House of Lords rejected it. Across the country people were outraged by this and riots broke out in many cities. The city of Bristol was controlled by rioters for three days. Nottingham Castle was burnt down and several people were killed at Derby. Leading Whigs became convinced that unless reform was introduced there would be a revolution in Britain. Finally, in June 1832, they were able to persuade the House of Lords to accept the changes and the Reform Act became law.

How was the election system changed?

The Reform Act changed the election system in a way that increased the number of electors and gave new MPs to many large towns.

Before	After
440,000 voters	720,000 voters
All voters were men	All voters were men
Many small towns had MPs while many cities did not	Large cities given MPs

Source B

The House of Commons 1833, *by Sir George Hayter.*

1 Look at the following list of causes of the Great Reform Act. For each one say:

a whether it was a long-term or short-term cause;

b how it helped to bring about the Great Reform Act.

- The Tory party had problems finding a good leader.
- The system of electing MPs was chaotic.
- Unemployment increased after 1829.
- Towns like Manchester had no MP.
- Organisations like the Birmingham Political Union were set up.
- There were riots in Bristol, Derby and Nottingham.

19 The Chartists

The 1832 Reform Act disappointed many working people because they still had no political power. Between 1836 and 1848 there were many different kinds of protest. One group of protesters called for a new, fair system of voting, and also for better living and working conditions. They were the Chartists.

Why did people become Chartists?

Gun fight in south Wales

On a wet Monday morning, 4 November 1839, the town of Newport awoke to the sound of marching men. Hundreds of people, mostly ironworkers and miners from the neighbouring area, marched in columns. They were carrying a variety of weapons, mostly home-made. These men were Chartists. They were on their way to the Westgate Hotel, where some local Chartists were under arrest. Guarding the prisoners in the hotel were some thirty soldiers, and outside were special constables. When the Chartists were refused entry, a fight broke out and some shots were fired into the hotel. One bullet hit the mayor in the hip. The soldiers were ordered to fire into the street. Twenty-two Chartists were killed; the rest fled in panic.

A modern artist's impression of the Chartist rising in Newport in 1839.

The Charter

Although such violence was rare, it still gives us an important insight into the Chartist movement. It shows us how strongly people felt about the issues behind the Charter. The Charter had been drawn up by some London working men in 1836 and was a demand for six important political reforms. The Chartists were Radicals who were bitterly disappointed by the 1832 Reform Act because it only gave the vote to relatively well-off men.

Source A

A Chartist handbill.

- *Why do you think the Chartists wanted each of these six points? Which of these six points is not the law today? Can you think of a reason why this is?*

The Six Points
OF THE
PEOPLE'S
CHARTER.

1. A VOTE for every man twenty-one years of age, of sound mind, and not undergoing punishment for crime.
2. THE BALLOT.—To protect the elector in the exercise of his vote.
3. NO PROPERTY QUALIFICATION for Members of Parliament—thus enabling the constituencies to return the man of their choice, be he rich or poor.
4. PAYMENT OF MEMBERS, Thus enabling an honest tradesman, working man, or other person, to serve a constituency, when taken from his business to attend the interests of the country.
5. EQUAL CONSTITUENCIES, securing the same amount of representation for the same number of electors, instead of allowing small constituencies to swamp the votes of large ones.
6. ANNUAL PARLIAMENTS, thus presenting the most effectual check to bribery and intimidation, since though a constituency might be bought once in seven years (even with the ballot), no purse could buy a constituency (under a system of universal suffrage) in each ensuing twelvemonth; and since members, when elected for a year only, would not be able to defy and betray their constituents as now.

In 1839, 1842 and 1848 huge petitions with millions of signatures were presented to parliament. Chartists went on strike and many were arrested, but the government refused their demands. The Chartists believed that they were asking for a fair and reasonable system, but to the government their demands were impossible.

● Why do you think that no government at this time gave in to the Chartists' demands?

Who were the Chartists?

Different groups of people supported Chartism for different reasons. The following sources give you examples of some of these reasons.

Source B

Leicester was a centre of Chartism. There, most Chartists were from the declining hosiery industry. One Leicester Chartist wrote to his father:

'Dear Father,
Spread the Charter through the land. Let Britons bold and brave join in hand. I write you these lines from the point of death. I must now inform you of the state of our town, we have had meetings every night this week. They assembled at night to the tune of 20,000 men or upwards and swore that by the ghost of many a murdered Englishman and Englishwoman, they would not stop until the People's Charter becomes the Charter of the land.'

From a letter by William Corah of Leicester to his father, 18 August 1842

Source D

A procession taking a Chartist petition to parliament in 1842.

Source C

Lancashire was also an area with a lot of Chartist support. This is an extract from an account by a man who travelled in the Burnley area of Lancashire in 1842, at a time of great unemployment:

'Groups of idlers stood in the street, their faces haggard with famine, and their eyes rolling with a fierce and uneasy expression. I found them all Chartists, but with a difference: the hand-loom weavers linked to their Chartism a hatred of machinery, which was far from being shared by the factory workers. The latter disapproved of anything like the use of physical force, while the former strenuously urged an appeal to arms. I heard some openly call for the burning down of mills.'

Cooke Taylor, *Tour of Lancashire*

● Why might hand-loom weavers and factory workers disagree about machinery?

Getting away from it all

Some Chartists tried to set up new villages where they could escape the grind and poverty of towns and live in harmony. The first of these was set up near Watford. It was called O'Connorville, named after a famous Chartist leader. None of the five villages was successful and the company running the scheme went bankrupt in 1850.

The decline of Chartism

After the third petition had been rejected by the government in 1848, Chartist support declined. Economic prosperity returned to Britain and, with unemployment falling, many people lost interest. Small groups of men continued to meet and argue for the Chartist reforms, but the days of the national movement were over. One Chartist leader, Ernest Jones, put forward his explanation for this.

Source F

'I believe that the less educated portions of the working classes feel little sympathy with political rights, unless they can be made to see the results in social benefits. There is little use in holding before them the Cap of Liberty unless you can hold the Big Loaf beside it.'

Ernest Jones, *Writings and Speeches*

● What is Ernest Jones' explanation for the decline of Chartism?

Source E

This is an extract from a Chartist speech:

'This question of universal suffrage [the vote for all men] was a knife and fork question after all. This question was a bread and cheese question. If any man ask him what he meant by Universal Suffrage, he would answer, that every working man in the land had a right to have a good coat on his back, a good dinner upon his table, and no more work than was necessary for keeping him in health, and as much wages for that work as would keep him in plenty.'

1 a Use all of the sources to list the different reasons why people supported the Charter.
b Sort your list of reasons into three groups: political, social and economic.

2 What do you think was the most important reason? Explain your answer.

The legacy of industrialisation

There were tremendous changes in the way people lived and worked in the period you have been studying. Factories were set up, new towns developed, the British Empire grew and there were many changes in the world of politics.

What links are there between this period and life today?

This factory presents an image of deindustrialisation.

In the nineteenth century, factories were set up in large parts of northern Britain. Since 1900 many of these factories and coal mines have gone out of business. These changes have caused unemployment and other problems in cities such as Glasgow, Newcastle, Liverpool, Manchester and Belfast.

Between 1750 and 1900 the number of men who could vote increased. However, at the end of the period some poor men and all women were not allowed to vote. The process of enlarging the electorate has continued during this century. Today, virtually all men and women over eighteen years of age can vote.

A woman, with her children, arriving to vote at a modern polling station.

Britain controlled a mighty worldwide Empire between 1750 and 1900. Almost all this Empire has now gone. Its impact lives on in the British people whose ancestors migrated from parts of the Empire to come and live in Britain. Many of the Caribbean islands and all of the Indian sub-continent were part of the British Empire, and many modern British people are of Caribbean or Indian descent.

● These are just three of the many links between changes made in the period 1750–1900 and conditions in Britain today. What other links can you identify? Look back over all your work and see what connections you can make.

This contemporary street scene reflects the multi-cultural nature of British society.

GRID

This grid is designed to indicate the varying emphases on attainment targets in the questions in each unit. It is not to be interpreted as a rigid framework, but as a simple device to help the teacher plan the study unit.

X   some focus
XX   strong focus
XXX   main focus

		AT1			AT2	AT3
		a	b	c		
1	Population growth and urbanisation	XXX		X		XX
2	Changes in farming	XXX	XX			XX
3	The birth of the factory		XXX	X		
4	Iron, coal and steam	XXX	X	X		
5	Canals, roads and railways	XX	XXX	X		
6	A worldwide Empire	X	X	XXX		XX
7	A trading nation	XX	X	XXX		XX
8	Child labour in mills and mines	XX		XX		XXX
9	Winners and losers				XXX	X
10	Squalor and splendour		X	XXX		XX
11	Religion	X	XX	XXX		
12	On the move		XX	XXX		XX
13	The role of women	XXX		XX		XXX
14	Growing up	XX		XXX		X
15	The real world of work					XXX
16	Power and the people			XXX		
17	The Peterloo Massacre		XXX		XX	XX
18	The Great Reform Act		XXX			
19	The Chartists		XXX			

INDEX